ISLAND COOKERY

Seafood Specialties and All-time Favourites

from Quadra Island British Columbia

**Quadra Island Child Care
Society**

Edited by: Star Weiss and Mary L. Pirie

Artwork by: Candy White

Front cover artist: Lorne Kask

Distributed by
Gordon Soules Book Publishers Ltd.
1354-B Marine Drive, West Vancouver, BC
Canada V7T 1B5
620-1916 Pike Place, Seattle, WA 98101, US
(604) 922 6588 Fax: (604) 688 5442
E-mail: books@gordon.soules.com

Copyright ©1981, by the
Quadra Island Child Care Society

Printed and bound in Canada by
D.W. Friesen & Sons Ltd.
ISBN 0-919537-01-4

First Printing 1981 - 2000 Copies
Second Printing 1982 - 5000 Copies
Third Printing 1982 - 5000 Copies
Fourth Printing 1984 - 5000 Copies
Fifth Printing 1987 - 3000 Copies
Sixth Printing 1991 - 3000 Copies
Seventh Printing 1995 - 2000 Copies

All proceeds to the Quadra Island Child Care Society
Quadra Island, British Columbia.

Printed on recycled paper

Acknowledgements...Island Cookery is a Quadra Island, community project sponsored by the Quadra Island Child Care Society to raise funds for the nursery school located in Heriot Bay.

However, even though nursery school parents compiled and produced this book, many other island residents also helped generously in the creation of Quadra Island's first cookbook. We'd like to thank the many, many people who made this book possible by donating their favourite recipes, and we're sorry that your overwhelming response made it impossible for us to include all, or even half, of the recipes we received for testing.

Our thanks especially to our Cookbook Committee, and to all the nursery school parents who helped during various stages of the work. Specifically, we'd like to thank all our recipe testers, and especially Robin Guldemond, Gail Devnich, Ann Minosky, and Charleen Clandening. Also thanks to all our typists, who worked with Donna Ludford and Cec Schnurr. A very special thanks to our typesetters Barb Gouge and Cec Schnurr, and to our artist, Candy White, who gave so much of their time to this project.

For proofing and layout help, we'd like to thank Penny Dowler, Jane Dowler, and Mieke Coddington. For the indexing, we thank Bob Moir, for his long hours of hard work, and for the use of her building for layout, our thanks to Sharon King. We also appreciate the help of any and all who babysat so that others could be working on the cookbook, since nearly 100 percent of those involved have at least one or two pre-school aged children. We'd also like to acknowledge Jessica Whittingham, for her generous help with editing and testing.

Finally, our deepfelt appreciation to our families, for their help and support throughout the project.

Last of all, we'd like to express our thanks and appreciation to Ann and Lorne Kask, for their hours beyond the call of duty in the preparation and printing of Island Cookery.

This book is dedicated to the children of Quadra Island.

TABLE OF CONTENTS

Metric Chart.. 2

Introduction... 4

Seafood Specialties...................................... 7

    Salmon, Cod
    Halibut and Others........................... 9

    Clams, Oysters, etc........................... 48

    Shrimp, Crab, Scallops, and Prawns................ 64

    Seaweed...................................... 75

All-time Favourites................................. 77

    Hors d'Oeuvres............................... 79

    Soups and Salads........................... 83

    Breads and Rolls........................... 93

    Main Dishes............................... 110

    Side Dishes............................... 157

    Sauces, Accompaniments & Beverages........... 163

    Desserts.................................. 173

Index... 208

METRIC CONVERSION CHART

The following metric chart is not exact, but is given in the most commonly used metric equivalents for imperial measures.

A NOTE OF CAUTION: If you use this chart for baked goods, remember that the key to success lies in keeping the proportion of the ingredients to each other in the same ratio as it was in the imperial measure.

Teaspoons

¼ teaspoon...1 ml.   2 teaspoons...10 ml.
½ teaspoon...2 ml.   2½ teaspoons...12 ml.
¾ teaspoon...3 ml.   3 teaspoons 15 ml.
1 teaspoon...5 ml. (surprise!)   4 teaspoons...20 ml.
1¼ teaspoons...6 ml.   5 teaspoons...25 ml.
1½ teaspoons...7 ml.

Tablespoons

1 Tablespoon...15 ml.   4 Tbsp...60 ml.
1½ Tbsp....25 ml.   5 Tbsp...75 ml.
2 Tbsp...30 ml.   6 Tbsp...90 ml. (for baked goods)
3 Tbsp...45 ml.   or 100 ml. (common)

Cups

¼ cup...60 ml. (the best equivalent for baked goods)
⅓ cup...75 ml.
½ cup 125 ml. (common)
        ...120 ml. (for baked goods)
⅔ cup...165 ml.
¾ cup...180 ml.
1½ cups...375 ml.
2 cups...500 ml. (common)
        ...480 ml. (for baked goods)
2½ cups...625 ml.
3 cups...750 ml.
4 cups...1000 ml. or 1 litre (common)
        ... 960 ml. (for baked goods)
1 cup...250 ml. (common)
        ...240 ml. (for baked goods)

Ounces & Pounds (Grams)

1 oz...28 g. (mass)
¼ lb...114 (exact)
    ...125 g.(common)
½ lb...227 g. (exact)
    ...250 g. (common)
1 lb...454 g. (exact)
    ...500 g. (common)..1 'generous' pound
2.2 lb...1 kilogram

Fluid Ounces (millilitres)

1 oz...28 ml.
    ...30 ml. (common)
10 oz...284 ml.

1 quart...1.1 litre
1.06 quarts...1 litre

Oven Temps.

Please note ALL oven temperatures in Island Cookery are given in degrees Fahrenheit (°F)

150°F......70°C.	425°F.....220°C.
250°F.....120°C.	450°F.....230°C.
300°F.....150°C.	475°F.....240°C.
325°F.....160°C.	500°F.....260°C.
375°F.....190°C.	525°F.....270°C.
400°F.....200°C.	550°F.....290°C.

To help you when you go to buy new pans or casseroles, the following chart is included. It is approximate, but should give you the closest size pan to buy to match your existing pans.

Cake pan...8 inch square....buy 2 L.
            or 20 cm. x 20 cm. x 5 cm.
            9 inch square....buy 2.5 L.
            22.5 cm. x 22.5 cm. x 5 cm.
            13 x 9 inch rectangular....buy 4 L.
            or 22.5 cm. x 32.5 cm. x 5 cm.
Layer cake pan...8 x 1½ in....buy 1.2 L. or 20 cm.
                9 x 1½ in....buy 1.5 L. or 22.5 cm.
Pie plate...9 x 1¼ in....buy 1 L. or 22.5 cm.
Casserole...1 quart....buy 1 L.
            2 quart....buy 2 L.

Introduction......

People who visit Quadra Island are often struck by the same thought...they have the feeling that life here is about 15-20 years 'behind the times.'

They point to things like our elaborate annual May Day celebration at Rebecca Spit Provincial Park complete with homemade neighbourhood floats, a May queen and court, Maypole dancers and a greased pole contest. Then they mention our community involvement, which includes such 'old-fashioned' activities as huge Nursery School dinners where all the food is donated and the entertainment is volunteer.

They marvel at a lifestyle where many residents choose to live without such modern conveniences as television, sewage systems, or even electricity. Finally, they point to the fact that our lives are slower, our hassles fewer, our friends somehow more loyal than ordinary.

Frankly, I don't know if we're 'behind the times' or not, perhaps we're ahead of them. But, in any case, it is true that Quadra Island offers its residents more than just a beautiful place to live. There is a definite sense of community on an island, probably because our boundaries are so obviously clear. We all live surrounded by the sea and that fact permeates our lives. What's more, many of us chose to live here specifically because we wanted the out-of-the-way lifestyle that islands offer. We moved here, not because of a job that uprooted our families, but because we were searching for an alternative.

We're willing to put up with a well that runs dry every few years, or a ferry line-up that forces us to spend an extra hour in town, if only we can spend summer evenings with friends on a Quadra beach.

4

So, about 2,000 of us choose to live here on Quadra Island, just a 10 minute ferry ride from the town of Campbell River. The Campbell River area, located on the northeastern part of Vancouver Island, British Columbia, is known as the 'Salmon capital of the World' and Quadra Island is an important part of the claim to fame. Sports fishermen from all parts of the globe make the trip to Quadra to try for the big ones (known locally as 'tyee' salmon). The abundance of our sea life influences what we do for a living and what we eat.

As for our social life, islanders usually consider a 'night out' as a night spent at a friend's house, most often gathered around a special meal.

We cook a lot for each other on this island and many islanders are famous locally for their superb cooking...

Tommy Hall's clam chowder, Mary's Mexican food, Mia's red pepper chowder, Pat's gourmet pears, Lorna's scampi, Russ' raclette, Judy's eggnog, Andy's pickled salmon, and Lorne's cataclysmic clams. More than normally, we know and enjoy each other's specialties.

It seems therefore, a logical progression to the creation

of this cookbook. In fact, the nursery school parents who eventually took on this project were not the first to seriously consider the benefits of compiling a collection of island recipes. Years ago, a group of friends, all members of the Quadra Old Age Pensioners Organization, decided to do a cookbook featuring their own favourite dishes. As the recipes were collected, Madge Nutting, an island resident since 1928, carefully saved them in an old chocolate box. There they stayed until a few months ago when Mary Pirie dropped into Mrs.Nutting's house to ask her for recipes for the cookbook.

By a great stroke of good luck, Mrs. Nutting's daughter-in-law Edith, who lives on the Nutting farm across the road, also dropped in and reminded Madge about the recipes collected years back. Out came the chocolate box and the recipes were turned over to Mary, with lots of helpful hints. Several of those recipes appear in this (the first) Quadra Island cookbook.

This is the sort of incident that has helped make Island Cookery become much more than just a nursery school project. The cookbook has involved people from all over our island, people who lead very different lives, but who shared an interest in seeing this community project succeed.

The result is a book which we feel accurately reflects the widely diverse and often unique cooking that you can find on our island. We've featured seafood, for obvious reasons, but our all-time favourites include so many creative ways to use food that we think you'll be surprised by it too.

We pretested over 600 recipes, and have presented only about 230 for you here. This was the hardest part of all for us...eliminating so many favourite dishes.However, we believe that the more than 200 recipes in this collection represent island cooking at its best. We think you'll agree.

S.W.

6

On Quadra Island seafood is both a specialty and a staple. Whether we're barbecuing a salmon on the deck for a dinner with friends, opening a can of smoked salmon to spread on crackers at Christmas time, or just trying to decide the best way to cook rock cod, the typical Quadra Islander eats...and enjoys...seafood all year long.

One of my favourite memories is of the night we roasted clams and oysters over a bonfire on the beach   in Hyacinth Bay and then watched the full moon rise over the waters of Drew Harbour, as we dipped our clams in garlic sauce and ate them on the half shell.

At certain times during the year we islanders get together at large social gatherings to enjoy seafood in style. There's the annual salmon barbeque put on by the Kwakiutl fishing families at Cape Mudge, where the salmon is cooked on cedar sticks, Indian style, over a huge open fire. Later everyone sits at picnic tables, on the grass, or on the beach to savour the tantalizing taste of cedar-scented salmon.

Another popular seafood gathering is the Legion seafood dinner. Islanders crowd in to consume a wide variety of seafood dishes including baked salmon, oyster stew, clam chowder, deep fried cod, octopus patties, fried abalone, prawns and crab legs.

Often one of our fish boats ties up at the dock in Q. Cove or Heriot Bay with fresh crabs or prawns for sale. You know then that you've got a treat ahead for dinner (once you get past the squeak of the crab as he's immersed in a pot of boiling water).

Seafood is shared generously among islanders. A call will come to urge you to drive right over and pick up some salmon. A friend will pass on to you a pile of clams, because 'we've got so many, and they're so good fresh.' A neighbour, just in from a fishing trip, will bring over huge, fresh prawns.

The bounty of the sea touches all of us on Quadra. Now we can share some of our seafood secrets with each other and with you. The following recipes represent a unique collection of West Coast seafood delights that we know you'll enjoy serving again and again.

Salmon is a rich, oily fish that, as you can see, can be prepared in an almost endless variety of ways. Whether baking or broiling, roasting or poaching, here are a few general hints to make preparing your fish a little easier.

When cleaning a salmon, the very last thing you should remove is the tail. It makes a convenient handle and if you've ever tried to cut the fins off a salmon after removing the tail, you'll know what we mean.

Probably the most common mistake made by the novice fisherman when cleaning a fish is overzealous removal of the bloodline along the backbone. The abdominal cavity is lined with a clear, cellophane-like membrane called the peritoneal lining. Whether freezing or cooking the fish, this membrane helps protect the flesh and seal in the juices. Ideally, the cavity of a fish should be completely blood-free.with the lining intact.

If you're cleaning your fish for canning, do not remove the backbone. After canning it becomes soft and totally edible, adding valuable calcium and other nutrients.

Here's a quick lesson in filletting: Lay the cleaned fish on its side on a table. Before you begin filletting, insert the knife at the back of the abdominal cavity (in the vent) with the blade facing the tail. Insert until you can feel the backbone. With the knife-blade on top of the backbone, draw the blade back to the tail. Turn the fish over and repeat. This procedure is called under-cutting. The thickest portion of the fish is from the vent to the tail. Under-cutting permits you to make a clean fillet all the way to the tail without the usual loss of meat at the back of the fish.

Now, insert the knife behind the head of the fish, on the top side of the spine, and draw the knife all the way down the length of the fish to the tail. You now have one fillet separated from the backbone. Without turning the fish over, insert the knife under the backbone behind the head and draw it down to the tail. Discard head, backbone and tail.

To remove the belly bones, use a short knife. Hold the fillet in your hand, bone side up. Insert the tip of the knife under 3 or 4 bones at a time, perpendicular to them,

9

and peel them off as you would peel and apple. You now have a beautiful boneless fillet!

Salmon will keep in the coldest part of the refrigerator for 2 days. It should be covered loosely with plastic wrap, or put in a plastic bag.

When you catch that 30-pounder, you'll probably want to freeze at least part of it. The fish may be left whole, filletted or cut into steaks. Use moisture vapour-proof wrapping or containers and exclude air to prevent spoilage. Seal packages tightly. Ideal storage temperature is -10°F, although most home freezers maintain a temperature of 0°F, which is usually adequate. Salmon can be stored in the freezer for 2-3 months.

Be sure you have removed all the blood and viscera from the abdominal cavity and washed it thoroughly prior to freezing. Once the fish has been frozen, the blood leaches into the flesh and cannot be removed.

A whole fish may be glazed before wrapping. This helps protect the fish and will extend its freezer life. To glaze, freeze the fish until solidly frozen. Dip the frozen fish quickly into ice-cold water. A thin coating of ice will freeze immediately on the surface. Repeat several times. Wrap the fish in freezer paper or seal in polyethylene bags.

Chinook [Spring] Salmon

SMOKED SALMON DIP WITH SOUR CREAM

Makes: 2 cups

2 c. smoked salmon, crumbled
1 c. sour cream
garlic and salt to taste
dillweed to taste

Mix all ingredients together. Refrigerate for one hour. Serve with chips, crackers or flatbread.

Mary-Lee Goodall

BILL'S SALMON DIP

1 small can (1/2 lb.) salmon
3/4 to 1 c. mayonnaise
1/3 c. sweet pickle relish
1/2 c. onion, chopped fine
dash salt and regular pepper
1/2 tsp. Lawry's lemon pepper (or coarsely
   ground pepper)
one eighth tsp. liquid smoke

Drain liquid from salmon. Separate salmon with fork, removing bones and skin. Using 3/4 cup mayonnaise, stir all ingredients together. Taste, and if desired, add another 1/4 cup mayonnaise. Refrigerate several hours. Serve with snack crackers.

Audrey Nelson

SALMON-CHEESE BALL

1 can (1 lb.) salmon or 1 lb. leftover cooked
   salmon
8 oz. cream cheese
1 tbsp. lemon juice
1 tbsp. grated onion
2 tsp. horseradish
¼ tsp. salt
¼ tsp. tabasco sauce
¼ tsp. Worcestershire sauce
½ c. chopped pecans or almonds
¼ c. chopped parsley

If using canned salmon, drain and remove skin and bones. Combine thoroughly salmon, cream cheese, lemon juice, onion, horseradish, salt, tabasco and worcestershire sauce. Chill covered at least 2 hours.

Combine nuts and parsley and spread on large piece of waxed paper. Form salmon mixture into a ball and roll in nuts and parsley. Place on a plate, cover and refrigerate until serving.

Can be made a day ahead. Very good with crackers or long french bread sticks.

Variation: Try using smoke-canned salmon. Terrific!

Pat Garland

Coho Salmon

12

SALMON CHOWDER

Serves: 6

This hearty soup is quick and easy, but will bring you lots of compliments.

1 large green pepper, chopped
1 large onion, chopped
1/4 c. oil
2 medium potatoes, peeled and diced
1 tin lima beans and liquid
1 tin carrots and liquid or 2-3 fresh carrots
    thinly sliced
water
4 c. milk
6 tbsp. flour
1 lb. can salmon, drained and broken into chunks
2 tbsp. dried parsley, fresh is even better if
    chopped fine

In a large pot, saute onion and green pepper in oil until soft. Drain lima beans and carrot liquid into a measuring cup and add enough water to make 1½ cups.

Stir into pot potatoes, beans, carrots, salt, pepper and water. Heat to boiling, cover. Cook over low-medium heat 20 minutes or until vegetables are tender.

Blend flour and 3 tbsp. water until smooth, stir into pot. Cook, stirring constantly, until soup thickens slightly. Add milk. Stir in salmon; heat to boiling again. Mix in parsley. Ladle into soup bowls.

Robin Guldemond

Ann and Lorne Kask live on a tiny one-house island just off April Point and , quite naturally, eat a variety and abundance of seafood...everything from abalone which they dive for, to cod which they catch right off their front wharf. They use seafood in original, tasty ways and in their spare moments can be found enjoying salmon (or rock scallops or ...) on an evening 'dinner cruise' on their sailboat 'Ptarmigan Stew'.

FISHERMAN'S SPAGHETTI

Serves: 4

1 pint jar of salmon
½ c. chopped onion
½ c. thinly sliced carrot
½ c. chopped celery
4 tbsp. cooking oil
1 can (14 oz.) tomato sauce
¼ tsp. oregano
¼ tsp. rosemary
¼ tsp. garlic powder
salt and pepper to taste
grated parmesan cheese

Drain and flake salmon reserving juices and mashing bones. Cook onion, carrot, and celery in oil until onion is tender. Add tomato sauce, flaked salmon, reserved salmon juice and seasonings. Simmer slowly for one hour. Serve over hot cooked spaghetti. Top each serving with parmesan cheese.

Ann Kask

LORNE'S SALMON CHOWDER

Serves: 6

2 cans tomato soup
1 can milk
1 quart tomatoes undrained
3 medium onions, halved or 6 small onions whole
2 carrots cut in 1 inch lenghts
2 celery stalks cut in 1 inch lengths
⅓ c. cooked rice
1 bay leaf
¼ tsp. sweet basil
1 - 2 tbsp. chopped parsley
1 can (1 lb.) salmon
6 thin slices cheddar cheese
6 medium mushrooms, sauteed in butter

Combine all ingredients except salmon, cheese and mushrooms. Simmer until vegetables are tender, approximately 30 minutes. Add salmon, leaving it in large chunks and heat through.

Pour mixture into a casserole dish. Arrange cheese slices over the top. Arrange mushrooms over the cheese. Broil in pre-heated oven until cheese melts, approximately 3 minutes.

Lorne Kask

Pat Garland could write her own cookbook...and some day she just might. You'll find several of Pat's recipes included in Island Cookery and every one of them got rave reviews from our recipe testers.

Pat explains her interest in cooking and baking by saying that she was the oldest sister in a family of six children. Quite naturally, she soon ended up doing all the family baking. At one point, Pat took a Chef Apprenticeship course, but found that she didn't enjoy cooking when it wasn't for her own family and friends. Now, ever since moving to Quadra three years ago, Pat contents herself with whipping up superb dinners for her guests and admits, 'Cooking is a passion with me.

Pat got this salmon dish from a Col. Kidd, who worked with her when she was with the Canadian government in Washington, D.C. Col. Kidd got homesick for salmon, had some Arctic Char flown in from the NorthwestTerritories, and gave Pat this recipe to use on her very first salmon dish. Pat says from that time on, she has loved fish.

TOMATO BAKED SALMON
Oven temp.: 425° and 375°
Serves: 6

This is one of my favorite ways to prepare a salmon. When I was first given the recipe I did not think tomatoes would go well with the fish, but it does, surprisingly, in this method.

>   5 lb. whole salmon
>   salt and pepper
>   flour for dredging
>   6 tbsp. butter, melted
>   1 onion, minced
>   1 clove garlic, minced or pressed
>   1 tbsp. Worcestershire sauce
>   2 large tomatoes, peeled and chopped or
>   1¼ c. canned, drained tomatoes
>   ¼ c. light cream
>   1 tbsp. butter
>   1 tbsp. flour
>   Brandy or liquer

16

Mix together salt, pepper and flour. Dredge salmon and place in greased baking dish. Bake for 15 minutes at 425°.

Add butter, onion, garlic, Worcestershire and tomatoes. Reduce heat to 375° and bake for 30 minutes, basting frequently.

Remove fish to platter and keep warm. Melt butter in a small sauce pan and add flour to make a roux. Then cook a few minutes on low heat. Whish in the cream and then tomato mixture. Heat gently. Add either brandy or some liquer like Grand Marnier or even a touch of vermouth to taste. When sauce is very hot pour over fish.

Serve with lemon wedges.

Pat Garland

OYSTER STUFFED SALMON

Oven Temp.: 450°
Serves: 4 to 6

5 to 6 lb. salmon
1 tbsp. savory
1/2 tsp. pepper
1/3 c. chopped onion
1 pint oysters
1/4 c. chopped parsley
8 c. toasted bread cubes
1 1/2 tsp. salt
6 slices bacon, diced
3/4 c. chopped celery
1/4 c. melted butter

Mix bread cubes and spices in a bowl, cover and leave at room temperature. Fry bacon, onion and celery together until transparent. Add liquid from oysters and chopped oysters, butter and parsley.

Cover and refrigerate for four hours, then toss both mixtures together. Place stuffing in salmon and close with small skewers. Place on foil lined pan, put bacon strips on top. Bake for 10 minutes per inch stuffed thickness of fish (about 1 hour).

Lorna Burnett

17

SALMON ON CEDAR STICKS, KWAKIUTL INDIAN STYLE

Two gracious ladies, Louisa Assu and Ruby Wilson, were kind enough to sit down and explain to me the method used by the Kwakiutl people at Cape Mudge when they barbeque salmon over the open fire. Salmon roasted this way is unusually delicious, light, moist, with a slight cedar taste. It's well worth the extra effort to build the proper fire and find the right sized cedar sticks.

> **Fresh salmon, 5 to 10 lbs. each (or larger)**
> **8 or more split cedar sticks, about 12-18 inches long per fish.**
> **1 'barbeque' or 'split'stick...about four feet long and 1-2 inches in diameter, with a split down the middle of it for about ¾ of the way (or three feet), and a pointed end to be stuck in the ground. (One split stick needed for each fish).**
> **Wire to tie the fish on the stick.**
> **Alder, cedar or maple for the fire.**

Optional:
> **Grated onions**
> **Vinegar**
> **brown sugar**
> **molasses**
> **lemon juice to rub on the raw fish if desired**

Procedure:

First, clean the fish from the back. To do this, slit the fish down the back. Take out the stomach by gently pressing your knife against the back bone. You'll need to slit down each side of the backbone, and eventually, take the backbone out. After the fish is cleaned, lie the belly flat, with the two sides flaring out.

Next, slide the flattened fish down the split in the split-stick, with the neck end at the bottom. Lay the fish down flat, with the meat (not skin) side facing up, and insert three or more (often, five are used) horizontal cedar sticks across the fish to support it. (All cedar sticks should

18

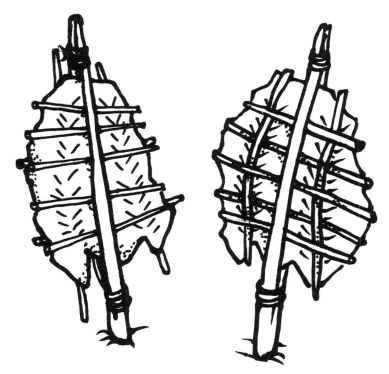

be inserted between the split-stick and the fish).

Turn the fish over and place two cedar sticks vertically on each flaring side of the fish, parallel to the big split-stick. Now, place three (or more) sticks across the fish on this side (the skin), and this time you will need to interweave the sticks with the vertical sticks, so that the top horizontal stick lies, for example, on top of the vertical sticks, the next horizontal stick lies under the vertical sticks, and so on.

At the top of the split-stick, tie a wire to secure the fish and sticks.

You are now ready to cook the fish, over the very hot coals of an alder, maple, or cedar wood fire. The split-stick can be either stuck in the ground at the pointed end, and leaned gently towards the fire, or you can tie a wire (or place a horizontal pole) to lean the split-stick against, as the fish begins its slow cooking.

The fish will need to have the meat side towards the fire

19

for much of the time, but you should turn it around for a while too, so that both sides of the fish are cooked through. It is hard to tell exactly how long you will need to cook your fish, depending on its size, but you should watch it carefully until you think its done, based on color and touch test. Usually, it takes about an hour for a large (15 lb. fish), so a 5 to 10 lb. salmon should take 45 minutes or so.

Finally, take the fish off and out, and enjoy a feast. Louisa Assu told me her family eats the salmon with eulachon grease. Ruby Wilson said that her mother used to rub the fish with grated onions before cooking, and that some families rub lemon juice, vinegar, brown sugar, or molasses on the uncooked fish, but many families use none of these extras, but simply cook the raw fish in the traditional style. Whichever way, its a delightful taste, and an interesting and enjoyable way to prepare a salmon on a special occasion.

Thanks also to Ida Assu and Joy Inglis for their help in explaining the process, so we could present it for you here.

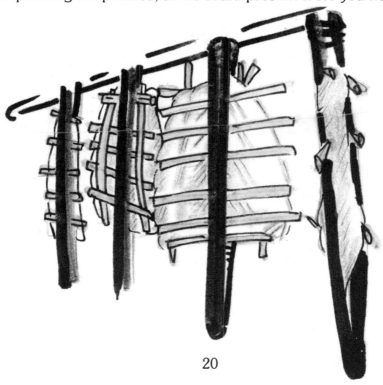

BAKED SALMON STEAKS IN SOUR CREAM

Oven Temp.: 450°
Serves: 5-6

2 salmon steaks or fillets approx. 2 inches thick
   (about 1½ lb. each)
oil (optional)
salt
1 - 500 ml. container sour cream
1 medium onion, finely chopped
1 tsp. dried tarragon or 1 tbsp. fresh
   tarragon or dill
2 tbsp. lemon juice
chopped parsley

Place steaks in a lightly greased pan. Brush lightly with oil, sprinkle lightly with salt. Bake about 25 minutes.

Add 1 tsp. salt to the remaining ingredients except the parsley. Mix well and spoon over steaks. Continue baking until fish flakes easily with fork, about 10 minutes. Sprinkle with parsley.

This is very elegant and tastes heavenly.

Mary Pirie

BROILED SALMON FILLETS

2 salmon fillets (use whole fresh salmon -
   about 6 lbs.)
½ c. ketchup
½ c. mayonnaise

Place fillets on broiling pan, skin side down. Combine ketchup and mayonnaise and spread thickly over salmon.

Broil 4 inches from element for 20 minutes. Serve immediately with lemon wedges.

Ruth Rombough

POACHED SALMON

salmon
thyme
pepper
white wine
parsley
1 clove

To one inch of water, add the above ingredients. Bring to a boil and simmer about 15 minutes. Place salmon steaks in at a very slow simmer (do not let it boil) on medium to low for 4 minutes on each side. Do not overcook. Take out of water immediately and serve.

Linette Wright Smith
(frequent visitor to Quadra)

SALMON TEMPURA

Serves: 4

2 lbs. salmon
2 eggs
1 tsp. minced parsley
1½ c. finely chopped walnuts

Fillet and skin salmon, then cut in 3 inch strips. Salt to taste. Beat eggs with 1 tbsp. cold water and parsley. Dip salmon in egg mixture, then roll in walnuts. Drop in hot fat and fry until golden brown, about 5-10 minutes.

Anna V. Joyce

SALMON

Fillet salmon and place on shallow baking dish. Cover very thickly with mayonnaise. Place under broiler approx. 6 inches and cook until mayonnaise is dark brown. Also you can use chopped onions.

Heather Vanderest

SALMON PIE

Oven Temp.: 350°
Serves: 4-6

1 can (1 lb.) salmon
2 c. soft bread crumbs
1/2 c. milk
1 egg, slightly beaten
1 tbsp. onion, chopped
1 tbsp. butter, melted
1/2 tsp. salt
spices of your choice; tarragon, dill etc.
4 potatoes, cooked and mashed
1 egg

Dill Sauce:
1 tbsp. butter
1 tbsp. flour
1 1/4 c. milk
1 tsp. sugar
3/4 tsp. dill weed
1/2 tsp. salt
1/2 c. sour cream
1 tbsp. lemon juice

Combine bread crumbs, milk, beaten egg, onion, butter and salt until crumbs are moistened. Add drained flaked salmon and mix thoroughly. Put in an 8 inch greased pie plate.

Combine mashed potatoes and egg. Spoon mixture around edge of pie. Bake for 30-35 minutes.

To prepare dill sauce, blend listed ingredients in melted butter, except for sour cream and lemon juice. Cook and stir until thick and bubbly. Combine sour cream and lemon juice then gradually stir into hot mixture. Serve wedges with warm dill sauce.   Ann Kask

SALMON MOUSSE WITH EGG SAUCE

2 c. cooked fresh salmon or 1 can (1 lb.) red salmon
2½ tbsp. fresh lemon juice
1 tsp. salt
dash cayenne
1 envelope unflavoured gelatin
½ c. cold water
3 tbsp. mayonnaise
¼ c. heavy cream

Sauce:
1 c. milk
¾ c. light cream
¼ c. whipping cream
2 small onions, sliced thin
½ bay leaf
1 whole clove
3 tbsp. butter
3 tbsp. flour
1 tsp. salt
dash white pepper
2 hard-cooked eggs

Drain salmon, discard bones, mash smoothly. Combine salmon, lemon juice, salt and cayenne.

Sprinkle gelatin over cold water to soften. Put in pan of boiling water and stir until gelatin is dissolved. Add to salmon mixture, then add mayonnaise, and the cream which has been whipped until it holds its shape. Pour into 1-quart mould and chill. Unmould on platter and garnish with watercress and deviled eggs.

Sauce:
Heat milk and cream together with the onion slices, bay leaf and whole clove until a film forms. Skim the surface.

Melt butter in a saucepan, stir in flour, keeping it smooth, and cook over a very low heat for a few minutes.

24

Pour in scalded milk mixture and cook over a low heat stirring constantly, until mixture bubbles. Remove from heat, season with salt and pepper, and strain into a saucepan. Add eggs, coursely chopped and heat through.

Do not cook any further. If the sauce seems too thick, add a little more light cream. Serve separately in a warm sauceboat.

The delight is in having the sauce warm with the cold mousse. Can add 1 tsp. tarragon to sauce for different flavour.

Donna Atkinson

SALMON CAKES

Serves: 4

2 c. water
1 tsp. salt
1/2 c. yellow cornmeal
1 lb. canned salmon
1 tbsp. chopped onion
1 egg
dash of pepper
1/4 c. flour

Combine water and salt and bring to a boil. Add cornmeal, stirring constantly until it thickens. Cover and cook over low heat for 10 minutes. Set aside and cool. Drain salmon, flake and remove skin and bones. Combine cornmeal mixture, salmon, onions, egg and pepper. Chill 2 hours. Shape into 8 medium-sized cakes. Dust in flour. Fry in hot fat, 5 minutes on each side.

These can also be made into patties, placed on cookie sheet and frozen for a quick meal.

Vyvyan Dorsett

SMOKED SALMON QUICHE

Oven Temp.: 350°
Serves: 4

1/2 c. mayonnaise
2 tbsp. flour
2 eggs, beaten
1 small can of home smoked salmon (5-7 1/2 oz.,
    or to taste. Don't overdo on salmon!)
8 oz. chopped swiss cheese
1/2 c. chopped green onions
1 unbaked pie shell

Combine all ingredients except pie shell. Pour into pie shell and bake for 40 to 45 minutes. Serve hot or cold.

Ruth Rombough

SALMON CROQUETTES

1 can (1lb.) salmon
2 c. mashed potatoes
1 egg
1 tsp. parsley
1/4 tsp. celery seed
1/2 tsp. salt
1/2 tsp. mustard powder
1 tsp. Worcestershire sauce

Mix above. Place one cereal spoon full on plate of cornmeal, and roll into a ball. Deep fry in fat until golden brown. Good with ketchup or mayonnaise.

Judy Odell

SALMON ROLL

Oven Temp.: 450°

Biscuit recipe, using 2 c. flour
½ lb. canned salmon
4 tbsp. milk
2 tbsp. lemon juice
1 tbsp. chopped onion
salt and pepper to taste

Make your favourite biscuit recipe and roll out on a floured board to ¼ inch thickness. Mix remaining ingredients and spread evenly over dough. Roll up jelly roll fashion. Bake for 30 minutes. Serve with egg sauce or white sauce.

Gladys Inrig

EVERYBODY'S SALMON LOAF

On an island of salmon fishing, there are always salmon dishes to think about. In the summer there are the leftovers from that great big baked salmon. In the winter there is frozen salmon and jars and cans of the lovely fish to use. Everyone loves salmon loaf, and the recipes poured in when we did our collecting for this cook book.

Here is a basic and excellent version followed by some variations and a few delicious sauces.

SALMON LOAF BASIC

Oven Temp.: 350°
Serves: 2

1 tin salmon (½lb.) or 1 cup fresh
1 c. bread crumbs
1 c. boiled milk
1 tsp. salt
1 tbsp. butter
½ onion, chopped
1 tbsp. lemon juice
2 egg whites beaten until stiff

Mix together all the ingredients, folding in the whites gently at the last. Bake for one hour in a greased casserole dish.

Deb Heath

SPROUT AND MUSHROOM SALMON LOAF

Oven Temp.: 350°
Serves: 4

2 (1 lb.) cans salmon
1¼ c. bread crumbs
½ c. milk
1 egg, beaten
1 onion, minced
1½ c. mung bean sprouts
2 tbsp. lemon juice
seasoning salt to taste
pinch of pepper
1 small can cream of mushroom soup

Soak bread crumbs in milk. Mix the remaining together and bake for ¾-1 hour. Great with baked potatoes.

Ruth Penner

We found many variations on the proportions used in the fish loaves. The results varied but most were excellent. Some people used as much as 1 quart of salmon or as many as three eggs. Everyone seemed to like lemon juice and parsley as flavourings. Some people preferred to separate the eggs and beat the whites. Some chose cracker over bread crumbs, very academic question! Basically, salmon loaf is a recipe to play around with, use up some leftover vegetables - you almost can't go wrong; especially with a nice sauce to go with it.

SIMPLE LEMON BUTTER SAUCE

Enough for 1 loaf

¼ c. butter
¼ c. lemon juice
dash of salt

Melt together. Pour sauce over salmon in pan or serve loaf and sauce separately.

Cec Schnurr

29

PIQUANTE SAUCE FOR SALMON LOAF

Makes: 1½ cups

2 tbsp. green onions, chopped
3 tbsp. butter
2 tbsp. flour
1 tsp. dry mustard
½ tsp. salt
dash of pepper
1¼ c. milk
1 tbsp. Worcestershire sauce

Cook onion in butter until tender but not brown. Add dry ingredients, stirring constantly. Add Worcestershire sauce and milk and cook over medium heat until thickened, stirring constantly.

Mary Pirie

EGG SAUCE FOR SALMON LOAF

Makes: 2 cups

2 tbsp. butter
1 to 2 tbsp. flour
½ tsp. salt
¼ tsp. pepper
2 c. milk
2 diced hard cooked eggs
2 tbsp. dried parsley flakes

Melt butter over low heat in saucepan. Blend in flour and seasonings. Cook over low heat, stirring until mixture is smooth and bubbly. Stir in milk, a little at a time, stirring constantly. Add parsley. Boil 1 minute. Stir in egg.

Robin Guldemond

We were deluged with everyone's favourite version of Pickled Salmon when we asked for recipes for this cookbook, so we've narrowed our choices to the following three variations. Lorna's is an oldtime favourite, Andy's is done without sugar and adds ginger and garlic and Gail's is a version that allows the fish to sit in salt brine for several weeks.

PICKLED   SALMON

salmon, approx. 6 lbs.
coarse salt
pickling spice
allspice
bay leaves
2 c. sugar
6 c. white vinegar
2 c. water

Fillet salmon. Put heavy layer of salt in the bottom of a crock (or some other large container), then a layer of salmon, alternating and ending with another heavy layer of salt. Put dish on top to weight salmon down. Refrigerate or keep in a very cool place for as long as you wish (at least 3 weeks).

Remove salmon from salt brine. Rinse and soak in plain water for 24 hours, changing the water several times. Then skin and cut into bite-size pieces.

Place a handful of the spices in a cheesecloth and combine with remaining ingredients. Bring to a boil and simmer for 25 minutes. Discard spices.

Layer salmon with onion slices, and occasional bay leaf, and whole allspice in jars. Cover with cooled boiled mixture.

Good after 3 days. Makes 2-3 quarts. Must be refrigerated.

Gail Devnich

31

Lorna Burnett has lived on quadra for more than 30 years, and has been making this version of Pickled Salmon for almost as long as she's lived here. She tells us it's a recipe from the Krook's family, who are also longtime residents, and says that 'all the oldtimers make it this way.'

When Lorna left her home on the Sechelt peninsula, she married into a Quadra fishing family, and her husband Doug is a well-known local fisherman. So, Lorna continued to perfect the seafood cooking she'd known for years, and she is noted for this recipe particularly.

PICKLED   SALMON

salmon, approx. 6 lb.
1½ c. coarse salt
1½ c. white sugar
3 onions, sliced
⅓ c. pickling spices

Skin and fillet salmon, then cut into bite-size pieces. Mix remaining ingredients together in a bowl.

Pack alternate layers of salmon and the onions and spice mixture loosely into a jar, then cover with cold white vinegar. Keep in fridge or very cool place. Ready to eat in 4 days.

Lorna Burnett

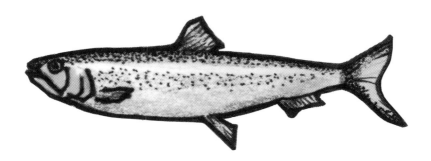

Pacific Herring

PICKLED SALMON

2 c. vinegar
2 c. water
1 tbsp. mixed pickling spice
2 medium cloves garlic, chopped
2-3 slices fresh ginger
1 lemon, thinly sliced
2 onions, thinly sliced

Clean and fillet a fresh or frozen salmon, removing the skin if desired. Wipe the fillet with a damp clean cloth; do not wash. Place salmon fillets in layers in a crock or other suitable container, salting each layer liberally with pickling salt. Let stand for 24 hours, then remove salmon and wash in fresh water.

The amount of brine needed will vary with the size of the fish. A good rule of thumb is to ascertain the volume of the jar or crock you will be using, and make ⅓ that amount of brine.

Mix the above ingredients except for the lemon and onion. Boil for 10 minutes, then cool.

Cut fish into bite-sized pieces. Pack salmon, onion and lemon into jar in alternate layers. Pour the cool brine over fish and let stand for two days in the fridge....if you can wait that long.

Andy Sitnik

Red Snapper

WARREN'S LOX

Salmon:
1/4 c. salt
1/2 c. brown sugar
2 tsp. crushed peppercorns
1 bunch fresh dill
3 oz. dill aquavite
board about 18x4x1 inch
large pan
3 lb. rock

Sauce:
3 tbsp. oil
1 tbsp. red wine vinegar
1 tbsp. sugar
1/3 tsp. salt
pinch white pepper
2-3 tbsp. prepared mustard
2-3 tbsp. minced dill
1 box flatbread or ryecrisp
1 bottle dill aquavite

Skin and fillet salmon, removing bone and wipe dry... do not rinse. Save the skin. Mix salt and sugar and rub each side of the fillet with half of mixture. Sprinkle on half the peppercorns and add half the fresh dill. Place the skin back on both sides. The fillets now look like a sandwich. You should have both fillets together - the belly side of one to the backbone of the other (the thick to the thin). Add half the dill aquavite. Place board on top of fillets and the rock on top of the board, refrigerate.

After six hours, pour off the liquid and refrigerate twelve hours. Now take the fillets, remove the skins and add the rest of the ingredients to the outside pieces, making them the inside pieces. Put the skin back on both sides and weight with board as before; twenty four hours is the minimum time...preferably forty-eight hours.

Sauce:

Blend together all ingredients except dill. Add the dill or serve from separate bowl. Take the skin and cut in long strips like bacon. Fry quickly and they will curl. Use these as garnish.

Cut the lox into bite-size pieces, dip into sauce and place on ryecrisp or flatbread and enjoy! Keep the dill aquavite in the freezer. Serve in frozen glasses (shot glasses)...now really enjoy!

Warren Peterson
April Point Lodge

SMOKED SALMON

Enough for 2 large fish.

1 c. brown sugar
½ c. coarse salt
½ tsp. pepper
1 tsp. garlic powder
½ tsp. paprika

Mix together all ingredients. Sprinkle over fish fillets and leave overnight. Rinse off and smoke.

Ferne Belanger

Cod is not only delicious and versatile, but has the extra advantage of being easy to catch. The lean, white flesh has a delicate flavour that lends itself easily to simple baking or something as exotic as Fish Kofta Curry.

There are many ways to clean and fillet a cod, and each individual has their own preference. Some people insist on cleaning the cod first, others feel it unnecessary. Some start slicing at the head, others at the tail, and there is a difference of opinion as to whether the first cut should be made from the spine down or the belly up. We are offering here one way to fillet a cod.

We advise leaving the fish whole, head and belly intact. Insert a sharp knife at the head behind the pectoral fin across the width of fish and draw it back to the tail without cutting through the skin at the tail. In other words, the fish is filletted on one side, but that fillet is still attached to the body of the fish by the skin at the tail.

Grasp the tail of the fish with the fillet away from you. Hold the edge of the knifeblade against the skin at the tail and pull the skin toward you, holding the knife still. You are, in effect, scraping the fillet off the skin. Turn the fish over and repeat on the other side.

Lingcod

MUSHROOM - YOGURT BAKED CODFISH

Oven Temp.: 400°
Serves: 4-6

A very simple recipe really but somehow slightly elegant. It is unusual and good enough to be a pleasant surprise the first time around. I use it often as my children are fond of it too.

2 lbs. cod, steak or fillets
6 tbsp. oil
¼ lb. sliced mushrooms
¼ c. butter
1 c. yogurt
1 tbsp. flour
½ tsp. thyme
salt
chopped olives (optional)
chopped green onions (optional)
chopped green peppers (optional)

Sprinkle fish with salt. Put oil in the baking dish, add the fish, turning to coat. Bake until tender. The time of course will vary depending on the thickness of the fish. It should be cooked just until it is no longer 'fleshy'.

Heat the butter and saute mushrooms until tender. Cover the fish with mushrooms. Blend yogurt with flour and crushed thyme until smooth and pour over the fish and mushrooms. Bake for another 15 minutes.

I almost always add the optional, particularly the olives and onions. Spread these on the fish along with the mushrooms if you are using them.

Jessica Whittingham

Madge Nutting has lived on Quadra since 1928, and her son and his family still farm the Nutting homestead. She and her friends started to assemble a Quadra cookbook several years ago, and thanks to Madge's careful storing of those old recipes, we are able to present a selection of them to you here in the island's first completed cookbook.

Madge tells us this recipe for sweet and sour island fried fish is from Alice Joyce, another Quadra old timer, and adds, 'It is good!'

ISLAND FRIED FISH

2½-3 lbs. cod, cut into 1½ inch cubes
Batter:
½ c. flour
½ c. cornstarch
1 c. milk
¼ tsp. pepper
1 egg
1 tbsp. baking powder
1 tsp. salt

Sauce:
2 cans pineapple, drained
½ c. vinegar
½ c. sugar
a few green onion and pepper flakes
1 - 11 oz. bottle of catsup
2 tbsp. soya sauce
2 tbsp. cornstarch mixed with a little
     of the pineapple juice
pineapple chunks, added last

Cut 2½-3 pounds of cod into 1½ inch cubes. Marinate for half hour in ½ cup soya sauce and ½ cup lemon juice.

Combine all batter ingredients together to consistency of heavy cream. Dip cod into batter and deep fry fish. Drain, arrange on platter and pour sauce over all.

Madge Nutting

COD FILLETS PIQUANTE

Oven Temp.: 400°
Serves: 4

¾ c. bread crumbs
2 lbs. Cod fillets
1 tbsp. vinegar
1 tbsp. Worcestershire sauce
1 tbsp. lemon juice
½ c. melted butter
1 tsp. prepared mustard
1 tsp. salt
¼ tsp. pepper
paprika to taste

Sprinkle the bottom of greased shallow baking pan with crumbs. Wipe fish with damp cloth and place in pan. Mix remaining ingredients and pour over fish. Sprinkle with paprika. Baste several times while baking.

Bake for 10 minutes per pound for fresh fish and about 20 minutes per pound for frozen fish.

M.E. Nutting

OVEN FRIED FISH FILLETS

Oven Temp.: 450°
Serves: 2-3

1 lb. fish fillets [sole, cod, etc.]
1 c. dry bread crumbs
¼ c. French dressing

Preheat oven to 450°. Cut fish in serving pieces. Dip in French dressing, then in bread crumbs. Arrange on greased baking sheet. Pour any remaining dressing over fish.

Bake for 15-20 minutes or until fish flakes easily.

Kay Dubois

39

FISH KOFTA CURRY

Serves: 4

2 lb. white fish
3 medium onions, sliced
salt to taste
1 bay leaf
2 green chiles
few parsley sprigs
2 tbsp. soft breadcrumbs
1 egg
½ c. butter
2 cloves garlic, minced
1 tsp. coriander
½ tsp. cumin
1 tsp. chili powder
¼ tsp. ginger
8 oz. tomatoes

Cook the fish in a little water with half an onion, salt and bay leaf until tender. Cool and remove, but keep the strained liquid.

Chop the green chiles and parsley leaves. Mash the fish and mix with the chiles, parsley, egg and bread crumbs. Shape into balls the size of a plum and fry in butter until brown. Drain and set aside.

Saute the remainder of the onion and garlic until golden. Add other spices and fry for about five minutes. Add chopped tomatoes and salt to taste and cook until tomatoes are mixed with the gravy. Add the liquid from the fish plus one cup of water and bring to a boil.

Put in fish balls and simmer 10 minutes. Serve with rice, a vegetable dish and pita bread.

Karen Murdoch

RED SNAPPER MEXICAN STYLE

Oven Temp.: 350°
Serves: 6

2 lb. red snapper fillets
1 large onion, chopped
1/4 c. oil (olive is nice)
28 oz. can tomatoes, drained and chopped
salt and pepper to taste
2 pimientoes, drained and coarsely chopped
2 tbsp. capers, rinsed and drained (optional)
1/2 c. pitted green olives, rinsed (optional)
generous amount of grated Monterey Jack cheese

Saute onion in oil until transparent. Add tomatoes, salt and pepper. Cook for 5 minutes.

Place fillets in a greased baking dish. Sprinkle pimientoes, capers and olives over fish. Pour tomato sauce over all. Garnish with grated cheese.

Bake for 30 minutes or until fish flakes easily.

Robin Guldemond

BAKED HALIBUT

Oven Temp.: 400°
Serves: 4

2 lbs. halibut pieces
1 tsp. salt
1/2 tsp. pepper
juice of 1/2 lemon
1/2 onion, chopped or green onion
grated cheese and bread crumbs (optional)

Sprinkle halibut pieces with salt, pepper, lemon juice and onion. Bake for 35-40 minutes. For the last 15 minutes, sprinkle the cheese and bread crumbs on top, if desired.

Lorna Burnett

HALIBUT (OR COD) STUFFED STEAKS

Oven Temp.: 350°

Serves: 4

2 large halibut steaks or
4 smaller cod steaks
1 c. cubed carrots
1 c. cubed celery
1/4 c. mushrooms
1 glass sherry
1/2 c. bechamel sauce
1/4 c. bread crumbs (buttered)
lemon juice

Cook carrots and celery in some butter until tender. Add mushrooms and sherry and let simmer one or two minutes. Drain off excess liquid and reserve. Then add vegetables to the bechamel sauce. Season with salt and pepper to taste.

Dry the fish steaks and sprinkle with salt, pepper and lemon juice. Place steak in buttered baking dish. Spread a layer of vegetables over the steak then top with the other steak. Sprinkle with the buttered bread crumbs.

Pour the reserved liquid around steaks and bake covered for 30-45 minutes.

You may use fillets instead of steaks.

Debbie Carpenter

HERB-BAKED WHITE FISH

Oven Temp.: 400°

chives
parsley
tarragon
salt and pepper
butter
fish

Skin and fillet fish. Place in a well greased shallow pan. Sprinkle with finely chopped herbs. Sprinkle with salt and small amount of pepper. Dot with butter and bake for 20 minutes or until done.

If fillets look too thick to cook in this amount of time, cut the fillet in half.

Heather Vanderest

CREAMY HERBED HALIBUT

Oven Temp.: 350°
Serves: 6

2 lbs. halibut fillets or cod
2 c. milk
¼ c. flour
½ tsp. garlic salt
¼ tsp. pepper
¼ tsp. thyme
dash of oregano
½ c. chopped green onion
butter
paprika
parmesan cheese

Place fillets in a greased baking dish. Dot generously with butter.

Thoroughly blend milk and flour, no lumps. Cook over medium heat, stirring constantly until thick and bubbly. Remove from heat and stir in salt, pepper, thyme, oregano and green onion.

Pour sauce over fish. Sprinkle with paprika and parmesan cheese. Bake 30 minutes or until fish flakes easily.

Robin Guldemond

ORIENTAL FISH SAUCE

Sauce:
3 tbsp. peanut or vegetable oil
1 tsp. sesame oil
½-1 tsp. grated ginger root
5 tbsp. dark soya sauce (Kikkoman)
1 finely sliced green onion

Combine oils and heat over medium heat. Add ginger. Stir and cook 1 minute. Add soya sauce and warm. Pour over steamed or poached cod or salmon. Garnish with onion. This is enough sauce for 5 or 6 cod fillets, or 5 lb. salmon.

Mary Pirie

STUFFING FOR FISH

Oven Temp.: 450°
Makes: approx. 3 cups

2 tbsp. butter
½ c. diced celery
¼ c. chopped onion
2 tsp. grated lemon peel
½ tsp. salt
½ tsp. paprika
¼ c. sour cream
2½ c. bread crumbs

Saute celery and onion in butter until tender. Mix with other ingredients in a bowl. Rub cavity of fish with salt and stuff loosely.

Bake 10 minutes for each inch of thickness.

Hilda VanOrden

CRISP FISH BATTER

Fryer Temp.: 375°

⅔ c. cornstarch
1 tsp. vinegar
⅓ c. flour
1 tsp. baking powder
water

Combine cornstarch, flour and vinegar. Add enough water to make a medium thick batter. Heat oil to 375°. Add baking powder to batter. Dip fish chunks and fry 3-4 minutes.

Lorna Burnett

TUNA - TOMATO CHOWDER

Serves: 4

1 c. diced potato
1 can tomatoes
1 onion, chopped
1 stalk celery, chopped
3 tbsp. margarine
4 tbsp. flour
¼ tsp. pepper
1 tsp. salt
3 c. milk
1 can tuna

Drain tomatoes and chop, reserving juice. Combine tomato juice, potato, onion, celery and 2 c. water. Cook until tender, and set aside. Melt margarine, stir in flour and seasonings. Add milk gradually, stirring until thickened. Add to first mixture. Add tuna and chopped tomatoes and heat through.

Joy Bird

RED PEPPER CHOWDER

4 tbsp. butter
2 medium onions, chopped
½ lb. sliced mushrooms
1 tbsp. lemon juice
2 large red bell peppers, thinly sliced
2 - 14 oz. cans chicken broth
1 lb. new potatoes, sliced
2 tbsp. cornstarch
2 tbsp. water
1 c. sour cream
1½ - 2 lbs. sole; cut into bite-sized chunks
½ c. minced parsley
salt and pepper to taste
½ c. white wine or vermouth (optional)

Saute onions, mushrooms and bell peppers in butter until tender. Add lemon juice, broth and potatoes. Bring to a boil, cover and simmer until potatoes are tender. Blend together cornstarch and water. Stir in sour cream and add to soup gradually. Heat gently. Add fish to soup along with parsley and wine if desired. Cover and simmer just until fish flakes. Season to taste and serve.

Mia Frishholz

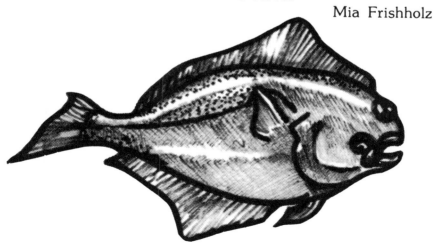

Halibut

CHEESE TUNA (OR SALMON) AND RICE MUFFINETTES

Oven Temp.: 375°
Serves: 6

A very good luncheon treat!

2 c. cooked rice
1 c. shredded cheddar cheese
1 - 6½ ounce can tuna, drained and flaked
   (or salmon)
¾ c. black olives, sliced into thirds
1 tbsp. minced onion
1 tbsp. parsley flakes
1 tsp. salt
2 eggs, beaten
2 tbsp. milk

Tangy Butter Sauce:
¼ c. melted butter
1 tbsp. lemon juice
½ tsp. salt (seasoned)
½ tsp. parsley flakes

Combine rice, cheese, tuna (or salmon), olives, onion, parsley and salt. Stir in eggs and milk, mixing thoroughly. Grease 6 muffin cups. Divide rice mixture evenly among cups. Bake for 15 minutes or until lightly brown. Serve with tangy butter sauce.

To make sauce combine all ingredients. Spoon over muffinettes.

Karen Abercrombie

Digging for clams is almost as much fun as eating them. There is a great deal of smug self-satisfaction in providing your own free dinner from the beach.

Clams, as with all mollusks, are best collected in the spring, fall and winter (or the months with an 'R' in them), since they spawn in the summer months, losing body fats and flavor.

To prepare clams for cooking, they must have a chance to 'spit' out all the sand they usually contain. Our first clam recipe details this process for you, which should be followed whenever fresh clams are used. Be sure all the clams you use are alive and tightly closed; discard any which have open shells.

Live clams can be stored in the refrigerator covered with a wet cloth for up to 24 hours. Shucked clams should be refrigerated in a tightly covered container with the strained liquor for no more than 1 or 2 days.

Frozen clams are a welcome convenience when you can't get out to dig, perhaps have missed the tide, or prefer not to brave some of our wintry Northwest weather. Always shuck clams (and oysters) before freezing them. It is possible to freeze raw clams, but this means shucking them is a bit more difficult. The preferred method on Quadra is to steam the clams open first, reserving the liquid from them, then packing them in freezer containers and covering them with the reserved liquid. Seal and freeze immediately.

Thaw frozen clams by placing the sealed container in a bath of cold water for a few hours, or letting them stand overnight in the refrigerator. Do not thaw them at room temperature, and never refreeze thawed clams.

In the interest of safety and good eating, it is advisable to find out before collecting any shellfish whether there is a red tide warning in effect. Though posters are usually prominently displayed in many areas, the best thing to do is to call the Fisheries Department in Campbell River for information.

LORNE'S CATACLYSMIC CLAMS

fresh clams
Sauce:
¼ c. clarified butter
1 tsp. finely minced onion or green onion
½-1 garlic clove, crushed
1 tsp. lemon juice
shake of salt
1 tsp. fresh parsley finely chopped

To make sauce, warm clarified butter in sauce pan. Then add remaining ingredients.

Put fresh clams into a bucket of sea water with a handful of rolled oats. Change water for cold fresh sea water after two hours. Let soak another couple of hours (use 3 times as much sea water as clams). Scrub clams thoroughly. Place in a steamer. Steam open over water with a tsp. of lemon juice added to it. When clams have opened place complete clam with meat portion down in lower ½ of shell on a cookie sheet or escargot tray. Spoon sauce over clam meat to fill each ½ shell. Place in hot oven for 5 minutes. Serve hot.

Option: A pinch of finely grated cheddar on top of each one.

Clarified Butter: Melt butter over low heat. When completely melted remove from heat and let stand for a few minutes, allowing milk solids to settle to the bottom. Skim butter fat from the top and place in container. This is the clarified butter.

Lorne Kask

CLAMS OR MUSSELS ON HALF-SHELL

Oven Temp.: 350°

    clams or large mussels
    butter
    garlic, freshly minced
    parsley, finely chopped
    bread crumbs
    dash of cognac
    tabasco
    Parmesan cheese

Steam clams or large mussels. Remove meat from shells and chop finely. Soften butter (estimate amount in relation to number and size of clams), mix with garlic, parsley, bread crumbs and dash of cognac. Place the above mixture back in half-shells. Sprinkle with a dash of tabasco and a liberal dose of Parmesan. Bake until warm and slightly browned.

Maureen Mather

CLAMS CASINO

Oven Temp.: broil

Use as many clams as you have the patience to open.

    uncooked clams (soft-shell)
    chopped onion
    chopped green pepper
    small pieces of uncooked bacon
    salt and pepper

Open uncooked calms. Leave in the half shell. Place clams on cookie sheet, and sprinkle on the bits of onion, green pepper, bacon, salt and pepper. Broil until bacon is crisp. Serve with your favourite beverage, but have a lot of napkins handy. Should be eaten from the shell.

Stephanie Webster

Tommy Hall came to Quadra when he was only a month old, and is one of the Island's true 'oldtimers' calling Quadra home for some 70 years. He fought the great fire that destroyed so many of the early settlers' homes, he ferried the passenger ferry for years, and he's a fisherman who knows how to put together a clam chowder which has been Island renowned for decades. Now, at last, here is Tommy Hall's clam chowder!

CLAM OR OYSTER CHOWDER

3 slices bacon or ham
2 medium potatoes
1 medium onion
1 tbsp. flour
2 c. water
2 c. milk
1/2 c. evaporated milk
1 tsp. parsley, chopped
1 tsp. salt
1/4 tsp. pepper
1 can oysters or clams, fresh or canned

Dice and half fry bacon or ham. Add onion chopped, and diced potatoes. Cook about 10 mins. stirring occasionally. Sprinkle with flour and stir to blend. Add water. Simmer until vegetables are almost done.

Stir milk in carefully; then add oysters or clams. Bring back to a simmer. Cook until vegetables are done. Pour evaporated milk in carefully and season with salt, pepper, and parsley.

Note: Diced carrots may be added with the vegetables if desired.

Tommy Hall

BOSTON CLAM CHOWDER

Serves: 4

½ lb. bacon, chopped
2 stalks celery, chopped
3 onions, chopped
1 green pepper, chopped
2 tbsp. flour
2 cans clams - 1 qt. fresh
2 c. tomatoes, quartered
2 potatoes, diced
1 tsp. parsley
½ bay leaf
thyme
salt to taste
1¾ c. cream or milk or 1¼ c. milk and ½ c.
    canned milk

Fry bacon until crisp. Add next three ingredients and saute. Add flour. Mix well. Add clams, tomatoes and potatoes. Bring to a boil. Add remaining ingredients except for milk and cream. Cover and simmer one hour. Just before serving add milk and cream and heat through.

Marjorie E. Nutting

CLAMS WITH BLACK BEAN SAUCE

fresh clams
Sauce:
2 tbsp. fermented salted black beans (not the
    canned ones)
2 tsp. minced garlic
2 tsp. minced ginger, fresh
2 tbsp. soya sauce
3 c. chicken broth
1 tbsp. cornstarch dissolved in ¼ c. water
2 tbsp. vegetable oil

Use half a pail of clams which have stood in sea water at least overnight to get rid of the sand inside. Scrub shells thoroughly and steam in small amount of water until open, no more than 15 minutes.

Rinse beans and pound to paste first 3 ingredients in mortar with pestle (or anyway you can). Then mix with soya sauce. Heat oil in wok or large heavy pan until it smokes. Add these ingredients and stir for 30 seconds. Then add chicken broth, reduce heat. When bubbling, add cornstarch mixture and stir until it thickens - now add drained clams in their shells and toss in mixture as you would a salad (they won't all fit in at once). Serve with garlic bread and a salad.

Olivia Rousseau

CLAM FRITTERS

Serves: 4

1 c. flour
1½ tsp. baking powder
salt and pepper to taste
¼ tsp. paprika
parsley to taste
1 or 2 small onions, chopped
¼ tsp. onion juice
½ c. cold chopped bacon
2 eggs, separated
½ c. milk
1½-2 c. steamed, shelled clams

Combine first six ingredients in a bowl. Add onions, onion juice and bacon. Beat egg yolks. Add milk to egg yolks and mix. Add milk and egg yolks to other ingredients and mix well. Fold in stiffly beaten egg whites. Add clams, stirring just to mix. Drop by tablespoonfuls into hot shortening. Fry until golden brown. Serve with desired fish sauce.

Alice Joyce

CLAM-MUSHROOM BAKE

Oven Temp.: 400°
Serves: 4

1 can baby clams, drained
1 can sliced mushrooms
¼ c. chopped onion
3 tbsp. margarine
2 tbsp. flour
½ c. milk
dash of Tabasco sauce
½ c. bread crumbs
2 tbsp. melted butter
1 tsp. parmesan cheese

Cook mushrooms and onions in margarine. Blend in flour; add milk and Tabasco sauce. Cook quickly, stirring constantly until thick and bubbly. Add clams. Pour into separate baking cups or shells. Top with crumbs, butter and cheese. Bake for 10-15 minutes.

Kay Dubois

For some people, an oyster isn't an oyster unless it's eaten 'pure' - that is to say, raw and untouched by sauces or condiments. For others, the symbol of seafood at it's best is Oysters Rockefeller. Whatever your preference, Quadra's oyster beaches can supply your basic ingredient.

Opening oysters can be a challenge to the novice. To open, hold the oyster with the deep half of the shell down. Insert a strong, blunt oyster knife between the shells near the hinge, and with a twisting motion, pry the shells apart. It's a good idea to wear gloves, in case the oyster knife slips and also to hang on to those sharp shells. Try to retain as much of the liquor as possible. Slip the knife between the opened shells and sever the muscle holding the shells together, then sever the under muscle holding the oyster to the shell. Remove any particles of shell.

54

Fresh oysters in the shell will stay alive in the damp atmosphere of the refrigerator for many days. Just be sure the shells are tightly closed before using the oysters. Discard any with open shells, and do not store oysters in water. Shucked oysters and the strained liquor may be stored in a tightly covered container in the refrigerator for up to 10 days.

Shucked oysters may be frozen after washing them in brine(1 tbsp. salt for each quart of water). Then drain and pack the oysters in freezer containers, covering them with the strained liquor. Seal tightly and freeze immediately.

Frozen oysters should be thawed overnight in the refrigerator or placed in a cold water bath for a few hours. Do not thaw them at room temperature and never refreeze thawed oysters.

HEARTY OYSTER STEW

Serves: 4-6

1/2 c. diced carrots
1/2 c. diced celery
1/2 c. butter or margarine
2 tbsp. all purpose flour
1 1/2 tsp. Worcestershire sauce
dash of bottled hot pepper sauce
2 - 10 oz. cans oysters
4 c. milk, scalded or 3 cups milk and 1 c. cream, scalded
1/2 c. sherry

Cook carrots and celery in 1/4 c. butter until tender. Blend flour, salt, Worcestershire sauce, hot pepper sauce and 2 tbsp. water until smooth. Add to vegetables. Add oysters and the liquid.

Bring to boil and simmer over low heat 3-4 minutes. Add hot milk, remove from heat and add 1/2 c. sherry. Cover and let stand 15 minutes. Heat a little and serve.

Hilda VanOrden

Since Hilda VanOrden moved to Heriot Bay 11 years ago, she has added seafood recipes to her repertoire, and has become known for such hearty seafood dishes as her 'Bongo Bongo' soup. When the VanOrdens give one of their memorable parties on the sprawling lawn in back of their seaside home, Hilda can usually be found in the kitchen fixing up one of her specialties.

BONGO BONGO SOUP

Serves: 4

2 c. milk
½ c. half and half
approx. 20 oysters, blanched and pureed
¼ c. cooked spinach puree
dash garlic salt
1 tsp. A-1 sauce
salt and pepper to taste
2 tbsp. butter
2 tbsp. cornstarch
1 c. whipping cream

Heat milk and half and half. Add oyster and spinach purees, seasonings and butter. Bring to simmering point but do not let boil. Thicken with cornstarch mixed with cold water. Simmer several minutes to allow cornstarch to cook.

Put into oven casserole, top with whipped cream and brown.

Hilda VanOrden

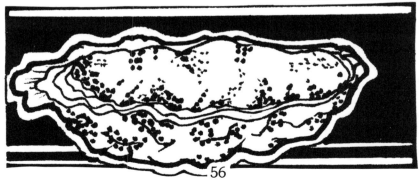

Hilda's Inauguration Stew is, we are told, based on the recipe for the stew which was served to the 'elite' passengers on the first trainride across Canada.

INAUGURATION   STEW

Serves: 4

½ c. butter
1 c. celery, diced
2 carrots, shredded
6 green onions, chopped
1 medium leek, sliced
¼ c. butter
½ c. flour
1 pt. milk
1 pt. milk (half and half)
1 can of clams, minced
1 pt. oysters
½ c. white wine or sherry

Combine first 5 ingredients in pot and simmer for 20 minutes. Make sauce of next four ingredients, season lightly, add to vegetables and set aside until ready to serve.

Bring clams just to the boil, add drained oysters and wine, stir over low heat for ten minutes, do not boil!

Add to the creamed vegetables and serve. You will enjoy!

Hilda VanOrden

FRENCH FRIED OYSTERS

This is my favorite way to eat oysters. French frying means dipped in flour, then egg, then bread crumbs. This recipe goes one step further in the addition of seasonings to those basic ingredients. Mushrooms, trimmed of stems work as well for this dish. Be careful you don't get small pockets of flour around the mushroom stems.

> **2 dozen oysters, shucked**
> **1½ c. fine dry bread or cracker crumbs**
> **⅓ c finely minced fresh parsley**
> **2 eggs**
> **2 tbsp. milk or cream**
> **1 garlic clove, minced**
> **salt to taste**
> **freshly ground black pepper to taste**
> **½ c. flour**
> **3 tbsp. each butter and oil for frying**

Clean oysters of any shell fragments and pat dry with towelling.

Combine the bread crumbs and minced parsley in a shallow bowl, tossing together well to evenly distribute parsley.

Beat eggs with milk or cream in a small bowl. Add garlic and some salt and pepper.

Add some salt and pepper to flour as well and put it in another shallow bowl.

Roll the oysters in flour, then dip in egg and then in crumb mixture. (Can be refrigerated at this point and fried later.)

Heat oil and butter in frying pan until bubbly over medium-high heat. Add a few oysters at a time and cook until golden on each side. Keep warm in the oven while frying the remainder.

Serve hot with homemade tartar sauce or a tomato sauce

and grated parmesan. Garnish with lemon wedges.

These oysters can also be used in an oyster sandwich. Slice fresh French bread rolls in half, butter them and spread with tartar sauce or mayonnaise. Put 2-3 fried breaded oysters on each roll, some lettuce, sliced tomato and whatever else you like. Top with the other bread half. Garnish with lemon wedges.

Pat Garland

CURRIED OYSTERS AND CORN

Oven Temp.: 350°
Serves: 4

1 lb. oysters
2 tbsp. oil
2 tbsp. butter
1/2 c. chopped onion
2 1/2 c. creamed corn
2 eggs, slightly beaten
1 1/4 tsp. curry powder
1/2 c. bread crumbs
1/2 c. grated cheese

Cut oysters into bite-size pieces. Heat oil and butter and saute onion and oysters about 4-5 minutes. Remove oysters and boil down remaining liquid. Add corn. Mix well. Place in small greased casserole. Stir in beaten egg, curry powder, oysters and corn and onion mixture. Cover with crumbs and bake 20-25 minutes. Sprinkle on cheese. Melt cheese in oven for a few minutes.

Hilda VanOrden

OYSTERS ROCKERFELLER

Sauce:
2 tbsp. butter
2 tbsp. flour
1 c. milk
1 clove garlic
tarragon to taste
fennel or anise, to taste
paprika to taste
salt and pepper, to taste
lemon juice
finely chopped mushrooms (optional)

Filling:
24 shucked oysters, on the shell
1 bunch spinach, finely chopped
1 c. grated cheese (mixture of mozzarella, swiss
   and parmesan)
½ c. fresh breadcrumbs
butter, cut into tiny bits

Make sauce by melting butter in small saucepan and adding flour. Cook this mixture over low heat for a few minutes. Whisk in milk and cook until thickened. Add garlic, spices to taste and mushrooms. Heat gently for 10-20 minutes.

To assemble: Put a bit of sauce on the bottom of each shell, then some chopped spinach, the oyster, more sauce, sprinkle on grated cheese and some breadcrumbs. Dot the crumbs with 3 or 4 bits of butter.

Broil about 6-8 inches from heat until cooked through and top is browned (20 minutes approximately).

Alice Brown

PAT'S HANGTOWN FRY

This was supposedly invented during California's Gold Rush Days and was a specialty of a place called Hangtown. It makes an excellent brunch dish. Good with broiled tomato halves.

> 6 medium sized oysters, cut up
> 4 tbsp. butter
> flour
> 4-6 eggs, beaten (depending on number of servings)
> 2-3 tbsp. cream
> salt to taste
> 1 tbsp. minced chives
> 1/4 c. finely chopped fresh parsley
> freshly grated parmesan

Dust oyster pieces in flour and fry until golden in hot butter in medium sized frying pan. Blend together eggs, cream, salt, chives and parsley and pour over oysters. Reduce heat to very low and cover. Serve when eggs are set. Sprinkle with parmesan and garnish with lemon wedges.

Pat Garland

KAY'S HANGTOWN FRY

1/3 c. oil
1/2 c. chopped green pepper
1/2 c. chopped carrot
6 to 8 medium oysters (shucked) patted dry
2 eggs beaten
1 dozen soda crackers, crushed fine
6 eggs
2 tbsp. milk
3 tbsp. minced parsley
1/4 c. grated Parmesan cheese
1/4 tsp. salt
pepper
lemon wedges

In large frying pan, saute carrot and pepper in oil until slightly softened. Remove from pan with slotted spoon. Dip oysters in two beaten eggs, then in crushed crackers. Fry in pan until golden brown. Meanwhile beat 6 eggs with milk, parsley, cheese, salt and pepper. Stir in vegetables and pour mixture over cooked oysters. Gently cook eggs by drawing in edges with a spatula, allowing uncooked egg to flow to the edge. When eggs are nearly set, put pan under broiler to brown very lightly. Serve with lemon wedges.

Kay Dubois

DEEP-FAT FRIED OYSTERS

Fryer Temp.: 375°

flour
salt and pepper
1 egg, beaten
1 tbsp. water
fine, dry breadcrumbs

Drain shucked oysters. Dry with paper towel. Roll oysters in flour seasoned with salt and pepper. Dip into a mixture of egg and water. Then roll in fine, dry breadcrumbs. Fry in hot fat until golden brown; about 2 minutes. Drain on paper towel. Serve with tarter sauce.

Sharon Calwell

ABALONE

abalone
butter
egg, beaten
fine bread or cracker crumbs

Sauce:
2 tbsp. vinegar
3 tbsp. soya sauce (Kikkoman is best)
1 tsp. sugar
1 tsp. oil (safflower)
garlic powder (optional)

Lay abalone on its back until it extends its foot out the side of the shell. Quickly insert knife and cut the base of the foot from the shell, cutting as close to the shell as possible. The entrails will remian behind in the shell. Trim upper black 'skirt' from around the perimeter of the foot. Using a stiff brush, scrub all black from the perimeter of the foot. Using a wooden mallet, pound the abalone until tender.

After tenderizing abalone, slice approx. ¼ inch thick. Saute in butter one minute each side or dip in beaten egg, then fine bread or cracker crumbs, then fry in butter. Option: can salt both sides. Serve with sauce:

Ann Kask

63

SHRIMP, HAM AND CHEESE SPREAD

Shrimp Spread:
2 lbs. (3 cans) shrimp
juice of 1 lemon
1 onion, grated
1 tsp. curry
3/4 c. mayonnaise
salt and pepper

Ham Spread:
1 lb. ham (3 c.) minced
4 tbsp. mustard
1/2 c. mayonnaise
2 tsp. horseradish
1/2 tsp.Worchestershire sauce
dash tabasco sauce

Cheese Spread:
1 1/2 lbs. cottage cheese dry curd (1 1/2 containers)
1 tbsp. grated onion
3/4 tsp. salt
2 tbsp. chopped parsley

Layer each spread about 3 times in a cake mold lined with cheese cloth. Cover with the cheese cloth and chill over night. Serve with crackers.

Sue Davenport

SCAMPI SAN MARCOS

Oven Temp.: 450°
Serves: 4

2 lbs. Scampi, or very large shrimp
1/2 c. melted butter
1/2 c. olive oil
1 tbsp. Worcestershire sauce
1 tbsp. parsley
2 stalks green onions, trimmed finely and sliced
    from end to end
juice of one lemon
2 cloves garlic, crushed and chopped
salt and pepper
1 c. Hollandaise sauce (white sauce method)
1 c. whipped cream, unsweetened

Mix butter, olive oil, Worcestershire sauce, parsley, lemon juice, garlic, green onions, salt and pepper to taste; mix well.

Peel and devein Scampi, leaving tail attached; split down the back of each lengthwise, being careful not to cut through the Scampi. Spread open to simulate a butterfly.

Lay open Scampi side by side in a baking dish. Pour butter mixture over; bake in a hot oven 5 minutes, basting once every minute.

Blend Hollandaise and whipped cream together gently. Remove Scampi from the baking dish and arrange on the serving platter. Cover with Hollandaise mixture (now known as Sauce Mousseline). Place under hot broiler until brown.

Serve very hot with French bread, tossed green salad, green vegetables and rice.

Lorna McKintuck

SHRIMP CREOLE

Serves: 4

2 medium onions, chopped
2 cloves garlic, minced
2 medium green peppers, finely chopped
1 c. celery, finely chopped
¼ c. butter
1 c. water
2 bay leaves
1 tbsp. dried parsley flakes
1 tsp. salt
¼ tsp. cayenne pepper
2 - 8 oz. cans tomato sauce
2 c. cooked shrimp meat, fresh, canned or
    frozen-thawed

In large skillet, saute onions, garlic, green peppers and celery in butter about 5 minutes or until tender. Remove from heat, stir in tomato sauce, water, bay leaves, parsley, salt and pepper. Simmer 10 minutes. Add additional water if needed. Add shrimp. Bring mixture to a boil. Cook covered over medium heat 5 minutes. Serve over rice.

Robin Guldemond

APPLE SHRIMP CURRY

Serves: 4

1 large onion, finely chopped
1 clove garlic, minced
2 tbsp. butter
1 medium apple, chopped
2 tbsp. flour
2 c. stock
2 tbsp. curry powder
½ c. dry white wine
1 lb. shrimp or prawns

Saute chopped onion and garlic in melted butter. Add apple and sprinkle with flour. Stir to smooth out lumps. Slowly add stock, stirring gently. Add curry powder and mix well.

Allow mixture to simmer for one hour. Add white wine and shrimp. Simmer slowly for 15 minutes. Serve with rice or crepes.

Teresa Precious

RICH-WITH-SHRIMP CURRY

Serves: 4-6

1 cube chicken bouillion
5 tbsp. margarine
1/2 onion, minced
6 tbsp. flour
2 tsp. curry powder
2 1/2 tsp. salt
1 1/2 tsp. sugar
1/4 tsp. ginger
2 c. milk
4 c. shrimp
1 tsp. lemon juice

Dissolve bouillion cube in 1 c. boiling water. Melt margarine in a saucepan. Add onion and saute until tender. Stir in flour, curry powder, salt, sugar and ginger. Gradually add chicken stock and milk. Cook over low heat, stirring constantly. Cook until thick. Add shrimp and lemon juice. Heat through. Serve over rice.

Deb Heath

Taku Resort is located in Drew Harbour and features a sweeping view of Rebecca Spit and the coast of mainland B.C..Ray and Connie Ludford offer their guests full tourist and fishing facilities, including cabins, motel units, a trailer park, store, restaurant, and boat rentals.

From the seaside dining room of the Taku restaurant, chef Bob Rainey offers this seafood specialty.

SCALLOPS AND SHRIMP

Serves: 4

1 lb. scallops
1 lb. large shrimp or prawns, raw, peeled,
    and deveined
2 cloves garlic, chopped fine
1 medium onion, chopped fine
pinch of tarragon
2 oz. butter oil (clarified butter)
1/4 c. white wine
1 oz. brandy
1/4 tsp. salt
1/4 tsp. pepper

To prepare butter oil, melt 3 to 4 oz. (1/2 c.) butter in saucepan on stove. The melted butter will form three layers, the fat on top, the oil in the middle, and the solids on the bottom. Skim off fat on top. Then ladle off the middle layer, which is the butter oil, and put it in a frying pan to use.

Fry the onion and garlic in the butter oil on medium heat. Add the scallops and shrimp and saute for 5 minutes. Add wine, salt and pepper, and tarragon, and cook for 5 additional minutes. Add brandy and cook for 3 more minutes. Serve on white rice.

Bob Rainey, Chef
Taku Resort

SEAFOOD ELEGANT

Serves: 12

2 tbsp. butter
3/4 c. flour
1 tsp. salt
4 c. milk
3 tbsp. tomato paste
1 tbsp. lemon juice
2 tsp. Worcestershire sauce
2 cans mushrooms
2 tbsp. butter
1 lb. scallops
2 tins crab
2 tins shrimp
(fresh seafood is nicer)

Melt butter, add flour and salt. Stir in milk, cook until it thickens (white sauce).

Add tomato paste to sauce, add Worcestershire sauce and lemon juice. Saute mushrooms in 2 tbsp. butter.

Wash scallops, cook in water 5 minutes. Drain. Cut smaller if too large. Add shrimp, crab and mix into white sauce. Serve with rice.

Vyvyan Dorsett

CRAB AND AVOCADO SALAD

2 c. crab
1 tbsp. grated onion
1 tbsp. lemon juice
1 c. diced celery
salt and pepper
lettuce, avocado and dressing

Toss the crab, celery, salt and pepper, lemon juice and onion lightly with sufficient dressing to moisten. Serve on lettuce and garnish with sections of avocado.

Old Timer Recipe

FAVOURITE CRAB DISH

Oven Temp.: 350°
Serves: 6

$\frac{1}{4}$ c. butter or margarine
3 tbsp. flour
2 c. milk
2 tbsp. minced onion
$\frac{1}{2}$ tsp. celery salt
one-eighth grated orange peel
3 c. cooked crab meat
$\frac{1}{2}$ c. soft bread crumbs
1 tbsp. minced green pepper
1 pimiento, minced
dash of Tabasco
2 tbsp. sherry (optional)
1 egg, beaten
salt and pepper
1 tbsp. parsley
1 tbsp. melted butter

Melt butter or margarine in double boiler, stir in flour and milk. Cook, stirring until thick. Add onion, celery salt, orange peel, parsley, green pepper, pimiento, Tabasco and remove from heat. Add sherry, if desired.

70

Stir a little of the hot sauce slowly into egg, then stir egg mixture back into sauce. Add salt and pepper to taste. Add crab meat. Turn into a greased casserole, sprinkle with buttered crumbs. Bake for 20 minutes or until brown on top.

May Embleton

CURRIED CRAB IN BAKED AVOCADO
Oven Temp.: 325°
Serves: 4

1/4 c. butter or margarine
1 apple, chopped
1 small onion, chopped
1 clove garlic, crushed
1 tbsp. curry powder, or more
1/4 c. wholewheat pastry flour
1 c. light cream
1 c. chicken stock or milk
1 tsp. salt
dash of white pepper
2 c. cooked crab
4 avocados, halved and peeled
3 c. cooked rice (brown is nice)

Melt margarine in a saucepan and saute apple, onion and garlic until soft and tender. Stir in curry powder and flour and simmer 1 minute. Gradually add cream and chicken stock or milk. Stir sauce until it thickens, add salt, pepper and crab. Increase curry to taste. Simmer sauce for 10 minutes.

Spoon cooked rice in a casserole and place avocado halves on top. Heat for 5 minutes, just long enough to warm avocados; do not overcook. Spoon crab sauce into avocado halves and serve with condiments of chopped eggs, coconut, raisins, chutney and chopped peanuts.

We find that a sweet apple compliments the curry and brown rice adds a nutty flavor and is more nutritious.

Rick Schnurr

71

CREAMY CRAB SAUCE

Serves: 4 to 6

¼ c. butter
¼ c. flour
½ tsp. salt
½ tsp. prepared mustard
2 c. milk
12-15 ozs. frozen, fresh-cooked or canned crab
   meat
1 can sliced mushrooms, drained
3 tbsp. dry white wine
1 tbsp. lemon juice
few drops of Tabasco
dash of garlic salt
1 c. grated cheddar cheese

Melt butter in heavy sauce pan. Blend in flour, salt and mustard, add milk all at once. Cook and stir until thickened and bubbly. Stir in crab, mushrooms, wine, tabasco, lemon juice, garlic salt and cheese. Cook until cheese melts. Serve over rice.

Robin Guldemond

April Point Lodge and Fishing Resort is the oldest fishing resort on Quadra, and attracts guests from all over the world. Phyllis Peterson, who now runs the resort with her sons Warren and Eric admits she never expected April Point Resort to become the large operation it is today when she and her husband Phil built the lodge in 1946.

Well known guests like John Wayne and Bob Hope have been regulars at April Point, which offers its guests a full range of facilities, and accommodations varying from modest to deluxe. April Point's kitchen and dining room is also well-known, and from the kitchen Phyllis shared with us this favourite recipe.

CRAB AND MUSHROOM QUICHE

Oven Temp.: 375°
Serves: 4-6

1 cooked pie shell
2 tbsp. lemon juice
1 c. crab meat (approx. 2 medium crabs)
1/4 lb. swiss or cheddar cheese
3 eggs
dash of nutmeg
1 tbsp. flour
1/2 tsp. salt
1 c. cream
1 c. sliced mushrooms

Combine mushrooms and juice. Fill shell with layers of mushrooms, crab and cheese. Beat eggs, flour, nutmeg, salt and cream. Pour into the pie shell. Bake for 30 minutes or until brown.

A 10 inch quiche plate and crust would be perfect to contain this generous sized quiche!

Phyllis Peterson

73

DEEP FRIED PRAWNS

Fryer Temp.: 375°
Serves: 4

½ lb. prawns (fresh or frozen)
1 tbsp. soya sauce
2 slices lemon
⅔ c. cornstarch
⅓ c. flour
1 tbsp. baking powder
salt and pepper, fresh ground
1 tsp. vinegar
½ c. water

Remove the shells from the prawns. Mix the cleaned prawns with a little salt and pepper and soya sauce. Prepare a batter by combining the cornstarch, flour, vinegar, and baking powder with enough water to make a consistency like pancake batter. Make sure hot oil or deep fryer is 375° before adding the baking powder to batter. This is important; if the batter sits too long after the baking powder is added, too much gas (carbon dioxide) is lost and you will not get a crispy cooked prawn.

Dip each prawn into batter and then fry. After 1-2 minutes the prawns should be golden brown. Remove and drain on paper towelling.

Serve with sliced lemons or sweet and sour sauce with pineapple.

Karen Murdoch

Joy Inglis is an Island resident who knows how to gather and prepare local seaweeds in a variety of ways. Joy, an anthropologist, delights in the delicate taste of seaweed coated in an oil-sesame seed mixture and lightly browned, and she was also pleased to pass along the following ways to enjoy this nutritious food product.

SEVEN SEAS SALAD SPICE

A few leaves of green sea lettuce (Ulva lactuca)
$\frac{1}{2}$ tsp. mustard seed
$1\frac{1}{2}$ tsp. sesame seeds
$\frac{1}{2}$ tsp. poppy seeds
$\frac{1}{4}$ tsp. ground peppercorns
$\frac{1}{4}$ tsp. cayenne
1 tsp. dried tangerine peel, ground

Toast a few sheets of dried sea lettuce over a flame (carefully - burns like tissue). Crush. Add other ingredients. Grind with mortar and pestle if you have one. Store in empty spice container.

Seven seas salad spice is sprinkled over a salad of greens (and favorite additives such as tomato, egg, etc.), and tossed with a dressing of $\frac{1}{2}$ cup oil and $\frac{1}{2}$ cup lemon juice. Adapted from a Japanese recipe.   Joy Inglis

SEAWEED AND CORN

Indians ate seaweed and clams; pioneers ate corn. When they got together at the time a cannery was set up in Knights Inlet, they produced a cross-cultural delight. This is my modification of the standard recipe. We use home-made creamed corn instead of 'Royal City' as called for originally, and we reduce the amount of cream and seaweed.

a few leaves of purple laver seaweed
(Porphyra perforata)
approx. 8 oz. creamed corn
$\frac{1}{2}$ c. whipping cream
salt and pepper to taste

Snip dried leaves of purple laver with scissors into strands approximately one eighth inch wide and three inches long. Simmer $\frac{1}{4}$ c. of these for 10 minutes in water. Drain.

Combine corn, seaweed and cream in top of double boiler. Cook over boiling water until hot. Salt and pepper to taste. Serve.   Joy Inglis

SEA-DEVILLED EGGS

Sea lettuce (Ulva lactuca)
6 hard-boiled eggs
salad dressing
Dijon mustard
salt and pepper

Crush two leaves of dried sea lettuce. Gently boil the six eggs, cool, shell, remove yolks. Set whites aside. Combine the yolks with salad dressing, mustard, white pepper, salt and seaweed.

A note on processing and procuring seaweed:
Gather the brilliant green leaves of sea lettuce from the rocks at low tide in March and April. Wash only in sea water. Dry thoroughly, and spread out on paper towels. Can be crushed and stocked in salt cellars or spice containers. Use liberally in cooking as you might use crushed and dried parsley. Very high in iron, high protein, vitamins A, B, C and other elements.

Marcelle Lascelles,
aboard the sailing ship Wun Wey,
calling regularly at Quadra Is.

ULVA LACTUCA

All-time Favourites

We think you'll be surprised by the variety and originality in this section of Island Cookery. The hardest part of putting this book together was deciding which recipes to leave out, since we were flooded with everyone's favourites and couldn't possibly include them all in this, our first cookbook. Perhaps Volume II will appear someday...we certainly have enough delicious recipes leftover to do another volume at least.

So, what we've tried to do is to include a good selection of dishes which are just a bit different...they are recipes that you can't usually find in other books. We have looked for unique uses of foods...in dishes we could all make easily. Of course, we have also included a few old stand-bys that aren't so 'unusual', until you taste them. Bon Appetit!

MUSHROOM - ALMOND PATE

2 tbsp. butter plus 1 tbsp. olive oil
1/2 c. minced onion
3/4 lb. mushrooms, sliced
1 clove crushed garlic
1/2 c. ground almonds
1/4 c. ground thyme

Saute onion in butter and oil. Add mushrooms and garlic. Saute until mushrooms are tender and golden brown, about 10 minutes. Cool mixture and chop finely by hand or puree coarsely in food processor or blender. Add ground almonds, thyme and season to taste with salt, pepper and garlic.

If pate is runny, add more ground almonds or pumpernickel bread crumbs.

Marcia Wolter

STUFFED MUSHROOM CAPS

18 large mushrooms
2 tsp. oil
1 small onion, finely chopped
1/4 lb. ground beef
2 slices ham, chopped
1/3 c. sherry
1/4 c. bread crumbs
1 tsp. salt
1 tsp. garlic
1/4 tsp. pepper
1/4 c. parmesan cheese

Remove mushroom stems, chop finely. Place caps on cookie sheet. Heat oil, cook onion and beef. Add stems, ham and sherry. Add parmesan cheese and seasoning. Stuff caps and broil 2-5 minutes.

Mary-Lee Goodall

80

MARINATED MUSHROOMS

Serves: 6

These are delicious as an appetizer with raw vegetables or in an antipasta platter or as a garnish to a salad.

1 lb. fresh small to medium sized mushrooms
1½ c. water
1½ c. cider or white vinegar

Spice Bag:
4 cloves
4 peppercorns
¼ tsp. mustard seeds
½ stick cinnamon
pinch of dried rosemary
1 bay leaf
(1 tbsp. pickling spice can be substituted
**   instead of above spices)**

2½ tbsp. olive oil
¼ tsp. basil, crushed
¼ tsp. oregano, crushed
1 clove garlic, minced
pinch of thyme
¼ c. chopped fresh parsley
salt and pepper to taste

Wash mushrooms and trim the stems. Put them in a large pot with the water and vinegar. Put the spices in cheesecloth and tie securely with string. Add to pot. Cover the pot and bring to a boil. Let it boil for 5 minutes then turn off the heat and leave the mushrooms covered in the hot liquid for an hour or two.

Drain the mushrooms thoroughly, rinse them and pat dry with paper towelling. Put them in a bowl and toss them with olive oil, garlic, the herbs and salt and pepper. Put aside to marinate for several hours before serving. They can be served chilled or at room temperature.

Pat Garland

FESTIVE STUFFED EGGS

1 doz. shelled hardboiled eggs
1 large tin tiny or broken shrimp or
    equivalent fresh shrimp meat
1 tbsp. lemon juice
1/3 c. ketchup
2/3 c. mayonnaise
1/8 tsp. dry mustard
paprika
black or green olives or pimento

Halve eggs. Arrange whites on platter. Place yolks in bowl. Mash egg yolks, add shrimp, lemon juice, ketchup, mayonnaise, and mustard. Mix well with an electric mixer if possible.

Fill egg whites with yolk mixture. Sprinkle with paprika. Top with black or green olive slices or pimento pieces.

These eggs are my own recipe and are very popular. Whenever I ask the host or hostess, 'what can I bring?,' the answer is, 'your eggs!' I make dozens and dozens every year.

Robin Guldemond

APPETIZER CHEESE BALLS

1 lb. sharp cheddar
8 oz. cream cheese
4 oz. bleu cheese
Worcestershire sauce
parsley

Soften cream cheese and the bleu at room temp. Grate cheddar very fine, combine with the other cheeses. Add a dash or two of the Worcestershire sauce. Mix all together until well combined. Form into ball and refrigerate. When ready to serve, roll in finely chopped parsley. Decorate with stuffed pimento olives.

Will keep for at least two weeks in refrigerator. Serve with assorted crackers.

Peggy Fraser

HEARTY MEATBALL BEAN SOUP

Serves: 10

Meatballs:
1½ lbs. ground beef
1 tsp. salt
¼ c. grated onion
¼ c. bread crumbs
1 egg, lightly beaten
¼ c. tomato juice
¼ tsp. black pepper
¼ tsp. marjoram
¼ tsp. basil
¼ tsp. garlic powder

Soup:
1 c. dry white pea beans
5 c. water
1 tsp. salt
1 clove garlic, chopped
½ c. diced celery
½ c. grated cabbage
½ c. diced turnip
½ c. diced carrot
2 onions, sliced
4 c. beef bouillon or broth
1 - 28 oz. can tomatoes
1 bay leaf
1 c. small macaroni or broken spaghetti

Combine all the meatball ingredients together and shape into meatballs.

Place beans and water in saucepan, cover, boil for 2 minutes. Remove from heat and stand covered for one hour. Add salt. Return to boil, reduce heat, simmer covered for 30 minutes.

Brown meatballs, drain fat, reserving 2 tbsp.. Set aside meatballs.

Stir fry vegetables and garlic in reserved fat until golden brown. Add vegetables, garlic, broth, tomatoes, bay leaf to undrained beans. Cover and simmer one hour, stirring occassionally. Add macaroni and meatballs to soup and simmer a further 30 minutes. Correct seasonings to taste and serve.

Allow 3½ hours for preparation. This recipe will adapt to any type of fresh vegetable you care to use (ie. cauliflower and broccoli) in place of those listed. This soup is worth the preparation time! The recipe is fairly easy to half for a smaller family but it would keep well in the freezer for use at a later time.

Ann Minosky

CURRIED PEA SOUP

Makes: 6 cups

1 tbsp. oil
1½ tsp. curry or to taste
2 carrots, sliced
1 c. dried peas
3 chicken boullion cubes
1 clove crushed garlic
1 medium onion, sliced
5 c. water
2 stalks celery, sliced
1 bay leaf
1 tsp. sugar
pinch of thyme or rosemary
salt and pepper

Saute onion and curry in oil until limp. Add all the remaining ingredients and simmer for 1 hour or until peas are definitely cooked. Remove bay leaf, blend in a blender or push through a food mill if desired.

If your boullion cubes are stubborn, dissolve them in a small amount of boiling water before adding to soup or they may remain cubes forever!

Linda Ludford

85

CREAM OF CHANTERELLE SOUP

Serves: 3-4

Try to use good whiskey in this, Canadian Club is splendid. Sherry may be substituted if you prefer, I would say try the whiskey. It is slightly risque.

1 qt. fresh chanterelles (or 2 c. sliced)
3 tbsp. butter
3 tbsp. flour
2 c. chicken broth or vegetable broth
2 c. whole milk or cream
¼ c. good whiskey
lots of grated nutmeg
salt and pepper to taste
pinch of thyme

Saute sliced mushrooms in butter just until soft over medium heat. Add the flour and stir for a few minutes. Be careful not to burn. Add the chicken broth.

Allow to simmer gently over low heat for 5-10 minutes stirring frequently. Add the milk or cream and heat thoroughly. Don't boil if you can help it, but nothing dreadful will happen if you do. Now add the whiskey (or sherry). Grate in your nutmeg, salt and pepper and a pinch of thyme if you like herbs.

Note: I have a stash of chanterelles in my freezer which have been sauteed, then frozen. These work in the recipe fairly well. Of course you can use 'store' mushrooms but you will lose some of the exotic quality of the soup.

Jessica Whittingham

86

QUADRA 'USE UP THE GARDEN' BORSCHT

6 c. water
2½ lb. short ribs, cut-up (or pork hocks, etc.)
2 medium onions, peeled and sliced
3 stalks celery (or chard) in 1 inch slices
4 large beets, pared and sliced
4 carrots, sliced
1 bay leaf
1 tbsp. salt
1 c. grated beets
1 (5½ oz.) can tomato paste
6 tbsp. vinegar (or slightly less to taste)
1 head green cabbage
6 or more small steamed potatoes

The day before serving, place water, ribs, sliced onions, celery, sliced beets and carrots, bay leaf and salt in a large pot. Simmer, covered, approximately 2 hours. Add grated beets, tomato paste and vinegar. Simmer, covered approx. 20 minutes. Cool and refrigerate overnight.

The next day remove excess fat, if any, from surface and remove bones. Bring borscht to a boil, lower heat, and add cabbage cut in wedges. Simmer 20 minutes or until tender.

Place just cooked potatoes in large bowls, spoon borscht over top and if you wish sprinkle with dill and place a dill pickle and spoonful of sour cream on top. Salt and pepper to taste.

Heather Kellerhals

SIMPLE   GARLIC   SOUP

Serves: 3-4

6-8 cloves of garlic, minced
1½ qts. water
2-3 tbsp. butter
4-6 oz. spinach noodles, or other
grated cheese
fresh parsley
dash or two of cayenne
1-2 bay leaves
1 tsp. oregano

Saute garlic in butter until golden, not crisp. Add water and bring to a boil, adding bay leaves, oregano, cayenne and finally the noodles. Adjust seasoning with salt if desired.

When noodles are tender pour soup over grated cheese in individual bowls and add sprigs of parsley.

Lolly Sipes

QUICK-N-EASY   AVOCADO   SALAD

Serves: 2

1 medium sized ripe avocado
½ ripe (but not mushy) tomato, chopped finely
½ stalk celery, chopped fine
½ c. peas canned or fresh frozen
1 small tin shrimp
½ c. mayonnaise

Skin, pit and chop avocado. Carefully mix all the ingredients in a bowl. Spoon onto lettuce leaves. Sprinkle with seasoned salt and pepper. One avocado mixture generously serves 2. This recipe doubles or triples well.

Robin Guldemond

HOT COLESLAW

Serves: 6

½ white cabbage, shredded
2 onions sliced in rings
1 tbsp. butter
8 oz. pkg. frozen green beans
3 tbsp. parsley
1 tbsp. creamed horseradish
salt and pepper

Lightly cook cabbage in salted water. Drain. Fry the onion rings in butter until tender. Add cooked beans, parsley, horseradish, seasoning and cabbage. Mix well together and serve very hot on its own or as a tasty accompaniment to roast beef.

M.E. Nutting

VERY GOOD CABBAGE SALAD

1, 3 lb. cabbage, shredded
2 medium onions cut in rings
½ c. sugar
1 or 2 shredded carrots
Dressing:
1 c. vinegar
2 tsp. 'hot dog' mustard
2 tsp. celery seed
1 tsp. salt
¼ c. sugar
1 c. oil

Toss the cabbage, onion rings and carrot with ½ cup sugar and set aside.
Bring all dressing ingredients except the oil to a boil, then add the oil and boil for a half minute more.
Pour hot dressing over the cabbage mixture. Mix well. Put into a bean pot or other suitable container.
Stores in fridge for 4-5 weeks.

Joy Inglis

89

MIA'S LOVELY LAYERED SALAD

Serves: 8

1 head lettuce, chopped
1 c. diced celery
1 small box frozen peas
1 sweet onion, sliced in rings
1 can water chestnuts, sliced
¾ c. mayonnaise
1 c. sour cream

Layer the above ingredients, except for mayonnaise and sour cream, in the order given in a deep (preferably glass) salad bowl.

Mix together mayonnaise and sour cream until well blended. Pour over salad, sealing right to the egdes of bowl with dressing. Refrigerate 12-24 hours. Garnish top with chopped hard boiled egg, crumbled bacon and grated cheese just before serving.

Mia Frishholz

MOLDED CHICKEN

1 envelope unflavored gelatine
2 tbsp. cold water
½ c. hot water or chicken stock
2 tbsp. vinegar
½ tsp. salt
1 tbsp. pimento
⅓ c. mayonnaise
pinch of pepper
2 tsp. sugar
1 c. cooked diced chicken
½ c. diced celery

Soak gelatine in the cold water, then dissolve in the hot water. Add the vinegar and salt and chill until partly set. Then add the remaining ingredients. Mold and chill. Serve on crisp lettuce with fruit such as grapefruit, orange, and avocado.

Old Timer Recipe

WILD   SPRING   SALAD

You can gather these herbs in late March and April to prepare this salad.

Some young Dandelion leaves
Chickweed
Water cress (it grows wild in ditches and wet
low lands)
Garden kale (which has wintered over)
Leeks (which have wintered over)
Violet leaves and flowers
Fresh chives
Fresh oregano

Chop all ingredients up finely and toss. You will have every vitamin and mineral that your body can use, plus iron and protein.

Jenny Calver

SUNSHINE   CARROT SALAD

Serves: 6

2 c. grated carrots
1 c. pineapple chunks
1 c. mandarin orange sections
$\frac{1}{2}$ c. raisins
$\frac{1}{2}$ c. grated coconut
$\frac{1}{2}$ c. raw or toasted sunflower seeds
4 tbs. yogurt, sour cream or mayonnaise

Mix all ingredients together. Serve on lettuce leaves. This salad is best when it is refrigerated 1 or 2 hours before serving. Great with pork or ham.

Carol Woolsey

HONEY DRESSING FOR FRUIT SALAD

1/2 c. sugar
1 tsp. dry mustard
1 tsp paprika
1 tsp. celery seed
1/4 tsp. salt
1/3 c. honey
1/3 c. vinegar
1 tbsp. lemon juice
1 tsp. grated onion
1 c. salad oil

Mix the first 5 ingredients. Add honey, vinegar, lemon juice and onion. Beating mixture constantly with electric mixer, slowly pour in oil. Store in refrigerator. Makes approximately 2 cups. Great in the summer.

Mary Pirie

Breads & rolls

TENDER SWEDISH WHITE BREAD

Oven Temp.: 350°
Makes: 2 loaves

2 c. milk, scalded
1 c. cold water
2 tsp. sugar
2 tbsp. yeast
4 tbsp. lard
4 tsp. salt
6 tbsp. sugar
1 c. potato water
9-10 c. flour

In a large bowl, combine milk and cold water. Remove 1 cup liquid to another bowl, to which you add the 2 tsp. sugar and the yeast. Let stand for 10 minutes, then add to large bowl.

Stir in lard, salt, sugar and potato water (water in which potatoes have boiled). Mix well.

Stir in and knead flour. Let rise approx. 1 hour or until double in size. Punch down. Shape bread into 2 rounds, brush with butter and prick with fork. Place on well greased cookie sheet. Let rise again, approx. 1 hour.

Bake approx. 30 minutes, or until brown.

Sherri Larsen

WHOLE   WHEAT   BREAD

Oven Temp.: 400°
Makes: 4-6 loaves

1 c. canned milk
4 c. warm water
1 egg
$\frac{1}{3}$ c. corn oil
$1\frac{1}{2}$ tbsp. coarse salt
$\frac{1}{2}$ c. lightly packed brown sugar
3 tbsp. yeast
7 c. whole wheat flour
7-8 c. white flour

Mix thoroughly milk, water, egg, oil, salt and sugar. Sprinkle yeast over mixture. Let yeast work in a warm place approx. 20 minutes. Beat well.

Stir in and knead whole wheat flour and white flour. Rise in well greased, covered bowl approx. 1 hour or until double in size. Punch down.

Divide into 4,5 or 6 loaves depending on size of pans. Grease pans well. Let rise again, covered, in warm place for approx. 1 hour.

Bake for 30 minutes. When done, rub margarine or butter over tops of loaves.

Gail Devnich

JENNY'S NEVER-FAIL RYE BREAD

Oven Temp.: 350°
Makes: 3 large loaves

3 tbsp. dry yeast
1/3 c. blackstrap molasses
1/3 c. oil
4½ c. vegetable waters blended with 1 c. cooked
   potatoes with skins
1 tbsp. sea salt
1/4 c. brewer's yeast
1½ c. bran flakes
1 c. wheat germ
1/2 c. unhulled sesame seeds
1 c. gluten flour
3 c. rye flour
3 c. whole wheat flour
For remainder of flour use unbleached white

Add molasses to 'potato water', sprinkle yeast on top and let sit 10 minutes. Add oil, salt, gluten flour then rest of ingredients, beating well after each addition. Beat in flour until dough is stiff then knead in more flour. Knead for 15 minutes, then let rise in greased bowl for 1½ hours. Turn out on board, knead briefly, divide into three parts and put into oiled pans. Let rise again for 1 hour. Bake for 45 minutes only.

You can vary the amount of potatoes up to 2 cups. The more potatoes the better the bread rises.

Jenny Calver

PILGRIM BREAD

Oven Temp.: 375°

1/2 c. cornmeal, yellow
1/3 c. brown sugar
1 tbsp. salt
2 c. boiling water
1/4 c. oil
2 pkg. yeast
1/2 c. warm water
1 tsp. sugar
3/4 c. whole wheat flour
1/2 c. rye flour
4 1/4 c. white flour

Dissolve sugar in warm water. Add yeast and leave 10 min. to 'proof' (yeast will foam).

Mix together cornmeal, brown sugar, salt, boiling water and oil. Cool to lukewarm. Add to yeast mixture.

Now add flours. First the wheat and rye, then the white. Beat with beater as long as possible. Then knead for 10 min., adding only as much flour as necessary to prevent sticking. Let rise until double, punch down, divide into loaves, rise until nearly double and bake 45 min.

Vera Millar

DILLY BREAD

Oven Temp.: 350°

Delicious warm from the oven!

1 pkg. yeast
¼ c. warm water
1 c. creamed cottage cheese (lukewarm)
2 tbsp. sugar
1 tbsp. dried minced onion (or 3 tbsp.
  fresh minced)
1 tbsp. soft butter
2 tsp. dill weed
½ tsp. soda
1 unbeaten egg
1 tsp. salt
2½ c. flour, approx. (white or a mixture of
  white and whole wheat)

Soften yeast in warm water. Stir in remaining ingredients, mixing well. Add enough flour (more or less the listed amount) to make a fairly stiff dough.

Let rise 50-60 min. in a warm place. Stir down. Turn into a well greased 2 qt. casserole dish or 2 loaf pans.

Let rise again 30-40 min.. Bake for 40-50 min. until golden. Brush with butter and sprinkle lightly with salt. Cool briefly, then remove from pan.

Linda Ludford

PULLA   (FINNISH   BREAD)

Oven Temp.: 350°

½ c. water
1½ c. milk, scalded
3 eggs
⅔ c. sugar
¼ lb. butter
1 pkg. yeast
½ tsp. cardamon, freshly ground
1 tsp. salt
1 c. raisins
8-9 c. flour (about 2 lbs)

Dissolve the yeast in ½ c. lukewarm water with 1 tsp. sugar. Let stand in a warm place for about 10 minutes.

Add butter to scalded milk and melt. Pour into large mixing bowl. Add sugar and salt. Mix well. Add 2 cups of flour. Mix thoroughly. Add eggs, then cardamon. Mix again. Add foamy yeast after the mixture has cooled to lukewarm or it will kill the yeast. Add raisins, then the rest of the flour one cup at a time.

Knead in bowl or on board until dough leaves your fingers. Add more flour if necessary. Put into greased bowl and turn it over. Cover and put into warm place to rise until double in bulk. Punch down. Knead again. Divide dough in half. Then divide each half into 3 equal pieces. Roll each piece into a strand. Braid 3 strands together. Either make it into a ring and put onto a greased baking sheet or make it into a loaf and place in a greased loaf pan. Cover and let rise until almost double. Brush loaf with beaten egg, sprinkle with sugar and chopped blanched almonds. Bake in moderate oven for 30-40 minutes.

Ann Kask

99

BAGELS

I had been making bagels for some time in Ontario - after eating them fresh from the bakeries of Kensington market in Toronto, but I did not find my own whole wheat flour variety to be quite what I wanted. On a walk in Toronto I came across the source of the Kensington Market bagels, and I went in for advice. Four cooks were busy cutting bagels by hand; shaping each one and cooking them in the old immense brick ovens. The bagels are stored in a refrigerated room on racks so they rise almost not at all, and they are boiled before baking, which makes them crusty.

Bagel dough can be made at night if you want them for a special Sunday breakfast, fresh from the oven.

3 c. mixed powdered milk
½ c. butter or margarine
½ c. honey or sugar
2 tsp. yeast
1 tsp. salt
2 eggs
whole wheat flour
1 egg, beaten
poppy seeds

Heat (but do not boil) milk, butter and sweetening until milk is scalded. Cool to lukewarm. Dissolve yeast in 1 cup warm water with a little sweetener. When milk mixture is lukewarm add salt, yeast mixture and 2 eggs.

Add enough flour to form a spongy mixture. Let it sit until it has risen slightly. Add flour until it becomes hard to mix with a spoon. Finish the process by turning it out on a bread board. Add flour and mix by hand until a firm but elastic and not too dry bread dough is formed. When the dough sticks to my hands just a little, I know it's firm enough.

Put it in a large oiled bowl. Put a damp cloth on top. Put

100

in refrigerator either overnight or 6-8 hours. It will rise some. Take it out and punch down. Form bagels the size of a medium lemon. Elongate by hand. Close the joint by rolling by hand. I do it in the air with one hand on each side.

Put bagels on oiled cookie sheet as you prepare them. Put completed sheets back in refrigerator as they are filled. Heat oven.

Heat a large pot of water to boiling. Put bagels in water, 4-6 at a time (depending on diameter of pot) for 10 seconds. Remove with a slotted spoon so water drains.

Spread each bagel with the beaten egg using a pastry brush. Sprinkle with poppy seeds. Bake 15-20 minutes or until medium brown and shiny on top. Best results in my oven come from a medium-dark cookie sheet.

Judy Odell

ZUCCHINI BREAD

Oven Temp.: 350°
Makes: 2 loaves

3 eggs
1 c. oil
2 c. sugar
2 tsp. vanilla
2 c. grated zucchini
1 can crushed pineapple, drained
3 c. flour
2 tsp. baking soda
1 tsp. salt
1/2 tsp. baking powder
1 1/2 tsp. cinnamon
3/4 tsp. nutmeg
walnuts, optional

Beat eggs, oil and sugar until foamy. Add vanilla, zucchini and pineapple. Sift together dry ingredients. Add to egg mixture and mix. Add walnuts. Pour into two well greased loaf pans. Bake for one hour or until they test done.

Nadine Mar

MEXICAN CORN BREAD

Oven Temp.: 400°

1 c. corn meal
1 tsp. salt
1 egg
1 c. creamed corn
1/2 tsp. baking soda
1/2 c. milk
1/4 c. oil
1 can green chiles
1/2 lb. cheddar, grated

Mix together corn meal, salt, egg and corn. Add soda, milk and oil. Wash and remove seeds from chiles. In well greased glass casserole, layer half the batter, then half the chiles, topped with half the cheese. Repeat. Bake for 20-25 minutes.

This is really a spoon bread and goes great with stews or chili.

IRISH BANNOCK

Oven Temp.: 375°

2 c. white flour
2 c. whole wheat flour
1/2 c. granulated sugar
2 1/2 tsp. baking soda
1/2 tsp. salt
2 tbsp. margarine
2 1/2 c. buttermilk

Put all dry ingredients in large bowl and mix. Mix in margarine with finger tips. Add buttermilk and turn dough out onto a floured board. Sprinkle flour on top of dough. Make dough into required shape on a cookie sheet. Cook for 45-50 minutes. Cool and slice.

Mary-Lee Goodall

SODA BREAD

Oven Temp.: 400° - 350°
Makes 2 loaves

5 c. whole wheat flour
1½ tsp. salt
2½ heaping tsp. baking powder
1¼ level tsp. baking soda
2 c. sour milk or buttermilk [approx.]

Combine all dry ingredients, mixing well. Add milk to make a fairly soft and sticky dough - similar to biscuit dough.

Turn dough out onto a floured surface and knead briefly. Divide into two round loaves and place both loaves on a greased cookie sheet (not touching). Make a surface cut across the top of each loaf.

Bake at 400° for 5 minutes; then lower the oven temperature to 350° and continue baking for approximately 30 minutes, or until golden brown. Remove from oven and cool on rack or tea towel. If the bread will not be eaten within a couple of days, it is better to freeze it so that it doesn't dry out.

Variations: If you wish, you may substitute 1 cup of bran, wheat germ or soya flour for 1 cup of the whole wheat flour. Other nice additions might be brewer's yeast, sesame, sunflower or pumpkin seeds.

Lorna Whyte

JEWISH COFFEE RING

Oven Temp.: 350°

1 c. butter
3 eggs
1¾ c. flour
1 c. sugar
1 c. sour cream
1½ tsp. vanilla
1 tsp. baking powder

Topping Mixture:
⅔ c. brown sugar
3 tbsp. chopped nuts
1 tbsp. cinnamon

Cream together butter, flour and sugar. Add beaten eggs, then flour, sour cream, vanilla and baking powder. Pour half of this batter into a greased and floured tube pan. (A springform one is best, but a regular bundt pan will do). Sprinkle ½ topping mixture on this, then add remaining batter followed by the remaining mix. Cut through mixture gently to marble it. Bake 50-60 minutes.

Nadine Mar

GOLDEN RAISIN BUNS

Oven Temp.: 375°
Makes: 1½ doz.

1 c. water
½ c. butter
1 tsp. sugar
¼ tsp. salt
1 c. flour
4 eggs
½ c. golden raisins (soaked 5 min. in hot water, then drained well)

104

Lemon Frosting:
1 tbsp. butter, melted
1½ tbsp. cream or canned milk
1 c. sifted icing sugar
½ tsp. lemon juice
½ tsp. vanilla

Bring water, butter, sugar and salt to boil. Add flour and beat until mixture leaves sides of pan. Remove from heat and beat 2 min. to cool. Add eggs one at a time, beating until smooth and satiny after each addition. Add raisins and mix well. Drop by measuring tablespoons full onto greased cookie sheet. Bake 30-35 minutes. Ice while warm. Lemon Frosting: Combine ingredients in order given.

Linda Ludford

APRIL POINT'S FAMOUS BRAN MUFFINS

Oven Temp.: 350°
Makes: 44

3 c. Bran Buds
3 c. sour or buttermilk
3 eggs
1 cup vegetable oil
1 c. white sugar
1 c. brown sugar
1 tsp. vanilla
3 tsp. baking soda
2 tsp. salt
3 tsp. cinnamon
Grated orange peel
3 c. flour
3 tsp. baking powder

Mix Bran Buds and buttermilk. Let stand for a few minutes while mixing the other ingredients in a separate bowl. Mix bran mixture with egg mix and fold in flour and baking powder. Don't over mix!

Put into muffin liners, ⅔ full. Bake for 15 to 20 minutes.

Phyllis Peterson
April Point

WHOLE WHEAT POPOVERS

Oven Temp.: 450°
Makes: 1 doz.

3 eggs
3 tbsp. oil
1 c. milk
½ c. white flour
½ c. whole wheat flour
½ tsp. salt

Beat eggs well then add oil, beat well and add remaining ingredients. Beat to the texture of unwhipped whipping cream. Lightly grease and flour muffin tins. Bake 15 minutes then lower oven to 350° and bake another 20 minutes. Pierce the tops of each with a fork to vent the steam. Test one for height and crispness. If not satisfactory, return to oven for 5 minutes. Serve immediately.

These are delicious and we prefer them to Yorkshire pudding, which they resemble, but without the smoking oil.

Mary Pirie

OATCAKES

Oven Temp.: 350°
Yields: 24

2 c. oatmeal (Millstream)
½ c. flour
1 tbsp. sugar
½ tsp. baking powder
½ tsp. salt
¼ c. butter or margarine or shortening
½ c. hot water

Mix dry ingredients together. Melt butter in hot water. Add and mix with dry ingredients. Roll out on slightly floured board. Cut with cookie cutter. Bake 25 minutes or until slightly brown. Cool.

Eat with butter and cheese or cold meat. Similar to Rye Vita (but better!).

Gladys Munro

COTTAGE CHEESE & YOGURT PANCAKES

Serves: 3-4

1 c. small-curd creamed cottage cheese
4 eggs
¾ c. flour
1 tsp. salt
maple syrup
1 c. plain yogurt
butter or margarine

Combine cottage cheese and eggs in small bowl with electric mixer. Beat at high speed until well mixed. Add flour, salt and 1 tbsp. syrup. Beat until smooth. With spoon gently stir in yogurt. Melt 1-2 tbsp. butter in skillet. Drop batter by rounded tablespoons into hot butter to form cakes 3 inches in diameter.

Bake on one side until browned and top is set, then turn and brown other side. Add butter as needed to prevent cakes from sticking. Serve hot with butter and maple syrup. Also nice served with warm apple sauce.

Very rich!

Carol Woolsey

107

SATURDAY MORNING WHOLEWHEAT BANANA PANCAKES

Serves: 2-3

1 c. whole wheat flour
3 tsp. baking powder
pinch of salt
one egg, beaten
1 c. milk
1 to 2 bananas

Mix dry ingredients well. Add beaten egg and milk mixture. Slice up banana on a hot buttered griddle, one slice per pancake. Quickly pour one ladle of batter over each slice of banana.

You may choose to use other fruit as well such as strawberries, peaches, pears, etc.

Russ Fuoco

LOVER'S WAFFLES

Serves: 4 - 6

2 c. whole wheat flour
3½ tsp. baking powder
½ tsp. salt
2 tbsp. sugar
2 eggs, separated
1¾ c. milk
4 tbsp. melted butter
1 tsp. vanilla
2 apples chopped to ¼ inch chunks or smaller

Sift flour with dry ingredients into a mixing bowl. Beat egg yolks, add milk, butter and vanilla. Gradually add liquid to dry ingredients and stir. Add chopped apples. Fold in stiffly beaten egg whites.

Pour batter in hot waffle iron leaving about an inch from all sides. Bake until mixture stops steaming. Don't peek!

Lorne Kask

GRANOLA DELUXE

Oven Temp.: 325°

A delicious 'everything' granola. Great as a snack or a cereal.

4 c. oat flakes
2 c. wheat flakes
1 c. soya bean flakes
1 c. wheat germ
2 c. sunflower seeds
2 c. coconut (flaked is best)
1 c. sesame seeds
1 c. bran
1 c. oil
1 c. honey
1 tsp. salt
2 c. dried bananas
3 c. raisins
2 c. chopped dried apricots (any dried fruit is good)
2 c. chopped nuts

Mix all the dry ingredients together (not including the dried fruit) in a large pot or bucket or whatever. Heat the oil, honey, salt mixture and pour it over the dry ingredients mixing well. Spread on cookie sheets to about the thickness of one inch. Bake for about 20 minutes, watching closely, stirring frequently, It will burn quickly when nearly finished. It should be golden brown. Now add the dried fruit.

Rene Archibald

Main dishes

SHASLIK OR SKEWERED MEAT KEBABS

Serves: 4

It is easier to cook all meat on separate skewers from the vegetables as cooking time varies. Though more attractive skewered together, it needs a bit more experimenting.

1-1½ lbs. of lean beef
quarters of tomatoes
green pepper
red or white onion
black and green olives
halves or slices of mushrooms

Marinade for beef chunks:
2 tbsp. lemon juice and rind (or more, to taste)
¼ c. oil
1 tsp. salt
dash of fresh ground pepper
½ tsp. turmeric
½ tsp. ginger
½ tsp. curry powder
2 pressed cloves garlic, or chopped finely
2 tbsp. apple cider vinegar or white

Chop meat into cubes, about 1-1½ inch are a nice size for skewers. Marinate over night or 2-4 hours, stirring over occasionally.

Thread meat on skewers; broil, turning a couple of times and basting with leftover meat marinade. Brush skewered vegetables with melted butter and lemon juice while broiling. Also, a bit of the meat marinade adds spiciness!

A very colorful dish to serve with a rice Pilaf and Pita bread.

Karen Murdoch

Mia and John Frishholz live in a unique, custom-designed home overlooking the sea on Francisco Point. Their spacious, open house features a locally carved totem in the living room, and is the setting for many dinner parties that are talked about on Quadra long afterwards.

Mia and John were first served this Nigerian Ground Nut Stew by a friend in Winnipeg, and, at the time, Mia was a week overdue with her first child. The morning after eating this dinner she went into labour, and she still attributes it to the spiciness of this dish. Her daughter Sarah was born within hours.

NIGERIAN   GROUND   NUT   STEW

Serves: 6-8

2 lb. ground beef
1 onion, chopped
¼ tsp. thyme
¼ tsp. oregano
¼ tsp. cayenne (or more)
2 small cans tomato paste
2 c. water
2 beef bouillon cubes
1 tbsp. Worcestershire sauce
½ c. ketchup
1 c. roasted peanuts
Condiments:
2-3 bananas
4-6 hard boiled eggs
1 green pepper
4 oranges peeled and cut up
1 cucumber
1 sweet onion
½ cantaloupe
1 large tomato
pineapple chunks
coconut
½ c. whole peanuts
remaining ground nuts
bowl of cayenne

Brown ground beef with onion. Add seasonings. Stir in tomato paste, water, bouillon cubes, worcestershire and ketchup. Simmer ½ to 1 hour. Half an hour before serving, add peanuts which have been ground in blender. Serve over rice in center of plate. Arrange condiments around the edge.

Mia Frishholz

ANDY'S CHILLI

Serves: 4

1 lb. ground beef
1 large onion, chopped
2 cloves garlic, minced
1 green pepper, chopped (seeds removed)
1 large banana pepper, minced (seeds removed)
2 one lb. cans kidney beans or equivalent
    amount prepared dried beans
1 - 2½ lb. can tomatoes
1 c. tomato juice or stale beer
2 boullion cubes
½ tsp. basil
½ tsp. oregano
½ tsp. cumin
½ tsp. thyme
1 tbsp. chilli powder, or more to taste
1 c. chopped ripe olives
salt to taste

Brown beef in a large pot adding a little oil if necessary. Add onion, garlic, and pepper when the meat is about half done. Add remaining ingredients and simmer, covered, at least an hour. If the chilli is made ahead and reheated, its better. Stir from time to time; taste it too. If it needs moisture add stale beer in preference to water. This is a flexible recipe in which ingredients can be varied any which way. Feeds even more if served over macaroni or rice. Goes super well with a big green salad, hard rolls and a modest red wine.

Andy Sitnik

MARY'S ENCHILADAS

Oven Temp.: 350°
Serves: 4-6

Sauce:
1 28 oz. can tomato sauce
1 14 oz. can tomatoes, chopped & undrained
1 tsp. brown sugar
$\frac{1}{4}$ tsp. oregano
hot sauce to taste (try jalapeno relish)
Filling:
1 lb. (2 c.) hamburger or chopped cooked beef or
chopped cooked chicken
$\frac{1}{2}$ c. ripe olives, chopped
$\frac{1}{2}$ c. green olives, chopped
1 med. onion, chopped
1 can green chiles, chopped (optional)
1 lb. sharp cheddar, grated
1 doz. corn tortillas
sour cream

Combine all sauce ingredients and simmer 10 minutes. If using hamburger, brown meat and drain fat. Whatever meat you're using, add enough sauce to moisten. Combine meat, olives, onions and chiles.

Assembly: Using tongs, dip one tortilla into hot enchilada sauce until it is soft and can be rolled without breaking.

Lay tortilla flat in a 9 x 13 inch pan. Fill center with meat mixture ($\frac{1}{4}$ to $\frac{1}{3}$ cup). Sprinkle very generously with cheese. Roll tortilla up and, if necessary, secure with a toothpick. Repeat until all tortillas are in the pan. Pour remaining sauce over all enchiladas. Top with remaining cheese.

Cover pan and bake for 30-40 minutes. Serve with sour cream.

These can be made vegetarian by leaving out meat and adding extra cheese or by substituting tofu for meat.

Mary Pirie

114

MUSHROOM-CHEESE MEATBALLS

Serves: 8

salad oil
¼ c. finely chopped onion
¼ c. finely chopped green pepper
1½ lbs. lean ground beef
1 egg
¾ tsp. salt
¼ tsp. cracked black pepper
½ lb. mushrooms, sliced
2 tbsp. flour
2 c. water
1 8-oz. package pasteurized process cheese
  spread, sliced
2 tbsp. cooking or dry sherry

In 12 inch skillet over medium-high heat in 2 tbsp. hot salad oil cook onion and green pepper until tender, about 5 minutes. In large bowl, mix well onion mixture, ground beef, egg, salt and pepper. Shape mixture into 1 inch round meatballs.

In same skillet over medium-high heat, in 3 more tbsp. hot salad oil, cook meatballs, a few at a time, until well browned on all sides, removing meatballs to large bowl as they brown. Pour off all but 2 tbsp. drippings from skillet. In drippings remaining in skillet over medium heat, cook sliced mushrooms until tender, about 5 minutes.

In small bowl, blend flour with water. Return meatballs to skillet; stir in flour mixture and cheese; heat to boiling, reduce heat to low; cover and simmer 15 minutes, stirring occasionally. Add sherry; heat through.

Donna Ludford

BAKED   MACARONI   &   MEAT

Oven Temp.: 350°
Serves: 6-8

1 lb. ground beef
1 medium onion chopped
small can tomato sauce
chopped parsley to taste
1/2 c. butter
3 tbsp. flour
lots of grated cheese to suit taste
mint to taste
salt and pepper
1 tbsp. catsup
8 oz. macaroni, uncooked
3 c. milk
5 eggs

Brown meat and onions in a little oil. Add tomato sauce, parsley, mint, salt and pepper and catsup. Simmer 20 minutes. Cook macaroni, drain. Stir in 1 tbsp. butter.

Make cream sauce as follows: melt remaining butter in a heavy saucepan. Add flour, then milk, stirring constantly until thick. Season to taste with mint, salt and pepper. Set aside. Beat eggs until thick and slowly add to the cream sauce.

Arrange half the macaroni in a greased baking dish. Pour half the sauce over it. Add all the meat mixture. Cover with remaining macaroni and then remaining sauce. Sprinkle liberally with grated cheese, then paprika for a nice color. Bake at 350° for 45 minutes until well browned.

Bev Juba

116

CHINESE EGG ROLLS

Serves: 4-6

Filling:
1 lb. ground beef (or diced beef or pork)
$1/4$ c. butter
4 c. finely chopped cabbage, partly cooked
$1/2$ c. finely chopped green onions
$1^1/2$ c. finely diced celery
2 c. bean sprouts
$1/4$ c. soy sauce
2 tbsp. sugar

Batter:
2 c. flour
2 tbsp. cornstarch
1 egg, beaten
2 c. water

Brown beef lightly in butter. Add vegetables and seasonings and cook about 5 minutes. Drain and cool.

To the sifted dry ingredients, add egg and sugar. Gradually beat in water until a smooth, thin batter is formed. Grease a 6 inch skillet lightly with oil. Pour about four tablespoons of batter. Cook over low heat until edges pull away from sides of pan. Remove from pan and cool. Place a heaping tbsp. of filling in centre of each pancake. Spread to within half-inch of edges. Roll, folding in sides, and seal with a mixture of one tbsp. of flour and two tbsp. of water. Fry egg rolls in deep hot fat (360-375°) until golden brown.

Mrs. H. Joyce

GOUGERE AVEC CHAMPIGNON

Oven Temp.: 400°
Serves: 6

A casserole using leftover chicken, ham or beef surrounded by a type of yorkshire pudding.

Pate a choux:
1 c. sifted flour
pinch salt and pepper
1 c. water
1/2 c. butter or margarine
4 eggs
1/2 c. diced cheddar cheese

Filling:
4 tbsp. butter or margarine
1 c. chopped onions
1/2 lb. sliced mushrooms
1/2 tbsp. flour
1/2 tsp. salt
1/4 tsp. pepper
1 envelope or cube instant chicken broth
1 c. hot water
2 large tomatoes (optional)
1 1/2-2 c. cooked chicken, turkey, ham or beef
  cut into thin strips
2 tbsp. shredded cheddar cheese
2 tbsp. chopped parsley

To make pate a choux:
  Sift flour, salt and pepper. Heat water and butter in large saucepan until butter melts. Turn up heat to bring water to a boil. Add flour all at once. Allow mixture to cook 5 minutes. Add eggs 1 at a time, beating well with wooden spoon after each one. Stir in diced cheese.

118

To make filling:

Melt butter in large skillet. Saute onion until soft not brown. Add mushrooms and cook 2 minutes.

Sprinkle with flour, salt and pepper; mix and cook 2 minutes. Add chicken cube and water. Mix well. Boil, stirring constantly. Simmer 4 minutes. Remove from heat. Cut tomato up into strips; add meat strips and stir.

Butter a 10-11 inch ovenproof skillet, pie pan, etc.. Spoon pate in a ring leaving centre open. Pour filling into centre and sprinkle all over with cheese. Bake for 40 minutes until gougere is puffed and brown, and filling is bubbling. Sprinkle with parsley and serve in wedges.

Carol Woolsey

STEAK SUPPER IN FOIL

Oven Temp.: 350°
Serves: 3-4

1½ lb. chuck steak, ½ inch thick
2 tbsp. water
1 small can cream of mushroom soup (10½ oz.)
1 envelope onion soup mix
3 medium carrots, quartered
2 stalks celery, cut into 2 inch pieces
3 medium potatoes, peeled and quartered

Place aluminum foil in baking pan. Place meat on foil. Stir together soups and water, spread on meat. Top with vegetables. Fold foil over and seal securely. Cook 1½ hours.

Meat becomes nice and tender and the gravy is delicious. Add a green tossed salad or a coleslaw and you have a lovely meal; nutritious and inexpensive.

Robin Guldemond

CHICKEN LEMONESE

Serves: 3-4

4 chicken breasts
1 egg beaten with 2 tbsp. water
½ c. white flour
½ c. grated monterey jack
½ c. grated parmesan
garlic powder to taste
¼ c. chopped parsley
1 tsp. paprika
salt to taste
3 lemons - juice of 2, 1 sliced
3 tbsp. butter, more if needed

Skin, bone and cut chicken breasts into serving pieces.

Put the egg and water in one bowl. Mix together the flour, cheeses and spices in another bowl. Drop chicken pieces into first the flour mixture, then the egg, then back into the flour cheese mix. Coat well. It may be necessary to beat another egg with water.

Melt butter in a medium hot skillet. Add a pressed clove of garlic for flavour. Saute chicken pieces in this, until golden brown on both sides. Remove from pan. Set aside.

To juices in pan add the juice of 2 lemons. Simmer briefly. Some additional butter may need to be added at this point if the pan is too dry. Add lemon slices. Serve the chicken with lemon slices and sauce from the pan.

This is very good with a rice dish or plain steamed rice and green beans with almonds.

Karen Murdoch

ANGEL WINGS

Oven Temp.: 350°
Serves: 4-6

This dish comes from Taxco, Mexico, where they call it Alas de Angel or Angel Wings. The sauce is angelic, and the breasts, when cooked, actually look like wings!

> **6 chicken breast halves, skinned**
> **3 tbsp. butter**
> **Salt and pepper**
> **1 c. chicken broth**
> **1 onion, chopped**
> **1 4 oz. can green chiles**
> **1 clove garlic, minced**
> **1 tbsp. flour**
> **$\frac{1}{2}$ c. cream**
> **$\frac{1}{2}$ c. shredded Cheddar cheese**

Brown chicken lightly in half the butter in a skillet and season with salt and pepper. Lay in a single layer in a greased shallow baking dish. Splash with about $\frac{1}{4}$ cup of the chicken broth. Cover tightly and bake for 20 minutes.

Sauce: Heat onion gently in remaining butter in the same skillet until soft and golden. Rinse, dry and seed chiles. Dice and add to the pan with garlic and flour. Stir and cook a minute or so. Add chicken broth (including any from the baking dish) to make 1 cup again. Stir over low heat until smooth and slightly thickened. Pour into blender and blend until pureed. Put back in skillet and add cream, stirring until simmering. Pour over chicken. Sprinkle with cheese. Bake for 25-30 minutes.

Pat Garland

CHICKEN IN WINE SAUCE
WITH DUMPLINGS

Oven Temp.: 375°
Serves: 4-6

3 lbs. chicken
flour
salt and pepper
2 chopped carrots
¼ tsp. thyme
¼ tsp. marjoram
1 clove garlic
a few mushrooms
1 onion
1 bay leaf
parsley
¾ c. white wine
¼ tsp. saffron or tumeric
2 tbsp. hot water
¾ c. sour cream

For dumplings:
¾ c. flour
1½ tsp. baking powder
1 tsp. salt
1 egg
3 tbsp. milk

Cut up chicken. Coat in flour, salt and pepper. Brown in butter, then place in a casserole dish with lid. Sprinkle with carrots, thyme and marjoram. In the same fry pan add garlic, mushrooms, onion, bay leaf, parsley and saute.
Add the wine, discard garlic and pour over the chicken. Cover and bake at 375° for 1 hour.
Stir saffron (or tumeric) with water and pour over chicken, then stir in sour cream.
Make dumplings by mixing flour, baking powder and salt. Mix egg with milk, then add to dry ingredients.

Put casserole on a medium temperature burner. At this point you may need to add a cup or two of chicken broth if there is not enough liquid to cook the dumplings. When the liquid is bubbling, drop in spoonfuls of dumpling batter. Cover for 15 minutes and serve.

Nadine Mar

JACK MAR'S FAMOUS CHICKEN WINGS
Serves: 3-4

1 package chicken wings (about 6-8 wings)
2 small crushed cloves garlic
2 tbsp. oil
¼ c. oyster sauce
½ c. chicken broth
2 green onions, cut in 1 inch lengths
2 tbsp. cornstarch
4 tbsp. water

Cut chicken wings at the joints and discard the tips. Heat oil in cast iron fry pan, arrange chicken pieces in fry pan and cook with fairly high heat (making sure not to burn). When they are done on one side turn them over and add garlic.

When they are done remove and clean the pan. Add a little oil and heat. Then put the chicken back into the pan. Pour the oyster sauce over the chicken and stir allowing the sauce to cook a little. Then add chicken broth, onion and bring to a boil. Thicken with cornstarch and water mixture and serve.

Can be served on rice or as an appetizer.

Jack Mar

CASTILIAN CHICKEN

Serves: 4

1 can (about 8 oz.) tomatoes
2 pounds chicken parts
2 tbsp. olive oil
1/2 c. finely chopped cooked ham
1 c. sliced onion
2 large garlic cloves, minced
1/4 tsp. pepper
1 can tomato bisque soup
1/4 c. dry sherry, optional
1 large green pepper, cut in 1/4 inch strips
1/4 c. sliced ripe olives
3 c. hot cooked rice

Drain tomatoes, reserving juice. Cut up tomatoes. In skillet, brown chicken in oil. Add ham, onion, garlic and pepper. Cook until onion is tender. Blend in soup, sherry and reserved tomato juice. Cover, cook over low heat 30 minutes. Add green pepper, tomatoes and olives. Cook uncovered 15 minutes more or until done, stir occasionally. Serve over rice.

Connie Ludford

CHICKEN IN WINE SAUCE

Oven Temp.: 350°
Serves: 4

2½-3 lbs. chicken
2 tbsp. butter
salt and pepper to taste
1 can cream of chicken soup
1 c. dry white wine
¼ c. heavy cream
½ c. shredded almonds
1 c. sliced mushrooms
2 tbsp. chopped parsley or dried flakes

Brown chicken slightly in butter, sprinkling with seasonings. Transfer to shallow baking dish, which will hold chicken pieces in one layer.

Combine soup, wine and cream. Pour over chicken. Sprinkle again with seasonings. Cover with foil. Bake for 30 minutes, uncover and bake another 30 minutes, or until tender, basting often with sauce.

Brown mushroom and almonds in butter. Sprinkle over chicken.

Danya Archibald

TERIYAKI OVEN FRIED CHICKEN

Oven Temp.: 400°
Serves: 4

1 c. soya sauce
1 c. dry white wine
¼ c. brown sugar
dash of powdered garlic or 1 clove minced
dash of powdered ginger or 2 slices fresh
dash Chinese 5 spice powder (optional)
chicken, cut up
4 tbsp. salad oil

Combine all ingredients and pour over chicken. Marinate at least 2 hours. Drain chicken well. Roll in flour. Pour oil in the bottom of a 9x13 inch pan. Place chicken in pan turning once to cover with oil. Bake for 30 minutes, turning once.

Mary Pirie

HOMEMADE SHAKE & BAKE FOR CHICKEN OR PORK

Covers at least one chicken

2 c. fine dry bread crumbs
¼ c. flour
1 tbsp. paprika
4 tsp. salt
2 tsp. sugar
2 tsp. onion powder
2 tsp. oregano
½ tsp. cayenne
½ tsp. garlic powder
¼ c. shortening (Crisco)

Combine all dry ingredients thoroughly. Cut in shortening. Store in tightly covered container in fridge.

E. Hooley

126

COMPANY BAKED FRYER

Oven Temp.: 375°

2½ lb. frying chicken, cut up
salt, pepper & paprika to taste
4 tbsp. butter
1 can drained & halved artichoke hearts
¼ lb. mushrooms, sliced
2 tbsp. flour
1 c. chicken broth
¼ c. dry white wine
½ tsp. rosemary

Sprinkle chicken with seasonings. Brown in butter. Remove chicken from pan and place in casserole. Arrange artichoke hearts between chicken pieces. Add more butter to pan drippings if necessary, and saute mushrooms. Sprinkle flour over mushrooms and stir. Stir in chicken broth, wine and rosemary. Cook until thickened, stirring constantly. Pour over chicken. Cover and bake at 375° for 45-60 min.

Joan Hope

GARLIC CHICKEN

OvenTemp.: 350°
Serves: 4

chicken pieces
2 cloves of garlic
½-¾ c. oil
vegetable salt [or salt and pepper]
2 c. wheatgerm

Pour oil into bowl and add salt and 2 cloves of garlic(chopped). Dip chicken pieces in oil. Pour wheatgerm in a plastic bag. Put oiled chicken (one piece at a time) in plastic bag and shake until well coated. Place in shallow pan. Bake for 1½ hours.

Diana DiCastri

CHICKEN ADOBO-[PHILLIPINO DISH]

Serves: 4

1 whole chicken, cut up into pieces
2 sections garlic, minced
½ c. vinegar
1 bay leaf
⅔ c. soy sauce
1 c. water

Put chicken in sauce pan and pour all ingredients over it. Cover and cook gently, stirring pieces from the bottom up to the top once or twice until the chicken is tender.

Remove chicken to a lightly greased frying pan. Pour a little bit of sauce over each piece as its frying. Keep adding sauce as it evaporates. If you add too much sauce at once the sauce will not coat the chicken. Save some sauce to spoon over rice or to use as soup base.

Jeannette Taylor

CHICKEN IN SOUR CREAM

Oven Temp: 350°

7 to 11 chicken breast halves or pieces
1 large can cream of mushroom soup (undiluted)
1 pkg. dry onion soup mix
½ pint dairy sour cream
1 tbsp. lemon juice
1 tsp. dill seed
Butter
Salt
Pepper
paprika

Place chicken breasts in buttered baking dish, skin side up. Dot each with butter, sprinkle with salt, pepper and paprika. Combine remaining ingredients and pour over chicken.

Bake in moderate oven for 1¼ to 1½ hours or until chicken is tender and sauce is brown. Serve with rice, green vegetable and tossed salad.

Lorna McKintuck

ROAST CHICKEN WITH DRESSING

Oven Temp.: 325°

1 large whole fryer, with giblets
2 cloves garlic, minced
1 large onion, chopped
1 large tart apple, chopped
½ c. pineapple chunks
½ c. thinly sliced mushrooms
¼ c. pimento stuffed green olives, sliced
2-3 tbsp. chutney
½ tsp. lemon thyme or regular thyme
salt and pepper to taste
dash of Worcestershire sauce

Remove giblets and heavy fat pieces from the cavity of the chicken. Wipe the bird with a clean damp cloth, inside and out. Wipe the outside with oil or butter and a slightly bruised garlic clove. Finely chop giblets. Heat chicken fat pieces in a heavy pan until melted. Add giblets, garlic cloves and onion. Saute until onion is transparent. Add remaining ingredients and a bit of cooking wine or boullion if moisture is needed. Spoon mixture into cavity of bird, sew or skewer shut, and roast in preheated oven until done. It usually takes over an hour, but test for doneness by twisting drumstick. If done, the joint is loose and all juices are clear, not pink. Also, about mid-way in the cooking, I cover the bird with tin foil to prevent over-browning. Serve with steamed rice and green salad.

Wendy Terral

129

MORRISON'S HAM PIE EXTRAORDINARY

Oven Temp.: 350°

Serves: 4-6

pie pastry for a double crust

2-3 c. chopped cooked ham or a closely
   equivalent amount of ham slices

2 tart apples thinly sliced

6 slices of bacon

1 onion, sliced

salt & pepper to taste

Line a pie plate with pastry. Cover with a layer of ½ of the ham, the sliced apples, the bacon, the onion and then the remaining ham. Complete with top crust. Brush with milk.

Bake until the crust is golden and you imagine the onions and apples to be cooked. Bake at 350° for about 45 minutes.

Charleen Clandening

BAKED PORK CHOPS IN SOUR CREAM

Oven Temp.: 375°

Serves: 4

4 loin pork chops ½ inch thick

4 cloves

3 tbsp. oil

enough flour seasoned with salt and pepper for
   dredging chops

½ c. water or stock

½ bay leaf crumbled

2 tbsp. vinegar or lemon juice

1 tbsp. sugar or honey

½ c. sour cream

¼ tsp. summer savory

Dredge the chops in seasoned flour. Insert a clove in each. Brown lightly in hot oil and place in a baking dish. Combine the remaining ingredients and pour over the chops. Cover. Bake for 1 hour.

Pat Garland

MU SHU PORK (SIMPLIFIED)
(MU SHU JOU)

½ lb. pork cutlet, or center cut boned pork chops
1 tsp cornstarch
1 tbsp. water
1½ tbsp. soy sauce
4 green onions
¼ c. peanut or corn oil
3 eggs, well beaten
2 c. shredded cabbage
1 tsp. salt

Cut pork into paper-thin slices, then into match stick strips 1½-2 inches long. (Slicing will be easier if pork is placed in freezer for about an hour). Combine pork with cornstarch, water and soy sauce; mix well. Cut onions into 2 inch lengths, then shred finely into thin strips.

Heat a large skillet or wok until very hot. Pour 1 tbsp. of oil into the skillet, then add eggs. Slowly push eggs back and forth until dry. Break cooked eggs into small pieces and transfer to a plate.

Reheat the skillet. Pour in the remaining oil. Add the green onions, stir-fry 30 seconds. Add the pork, stir-fry until it turns colour and separates into strips. If meat begins to stick to skillet add a little more oil. Add cabbage and salt, stir-fry over high heat for 2 minutes. Add cooked eggs, stir to heat through.

Carol Woolsey

131

SAUSAGE ROLLS

Oven Temp.: 400°

Crust:
4 c. flour
1 lb. margarine
1 - 10oz. can club soda

Filling:
2 lbs. good, fairly lean sausage meat
4 slices trimmed bread
1½ tsp. onion salt
½ tsp. garlic salt
2 tbsp. chopped parsley
1 tsp. pepper (or to taste)
1 tsp. poultry seasoning

Blend together the crust ingredients, cutting in margarine like pastry dough. Form into a ball and chill.

Soak bread briefly in milk, squeeze gently and tear into small pieces. Add to the remaining filling ingredients. Cook them all together in a medium temperature skillet until the sausage is cooked and then cool.

Roll crust dough into square, large enough to hold the spread out sausage meat. Make sure the crust is not too thick. Roll up like a jelly roll. Cut into the lengths desired. Brush with egg and milk for a glossy crust and bake 20-25 min. until golden and crispy.

Denise Langford

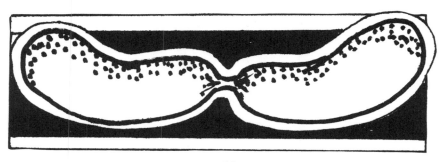

TERIYAKI SPARERIBS

Oven Temp.: 350°

⅓ c. soy sauce
⅓ c. honey
3 tbsp. vinegar
2 tbsp. sherry
1 tbsp. sugar
2 cloves garlic, crushed
1 tsp. powdered ginger
1½ c. beef broth (or consomme or beef bouillon)
2-3 lbs. spareribs

Mix all ingredients. Marinate spareribs for about 2 hours. Bake for 1 hour. Baste often.

Note: Marinating sauce can be kept in the fridge for one week without spoiling; it's good to use as extra flavour in sauces, gravy, casseroles, etc.

Mieke Coddington

Jenny and Richard Calver, who live in Quathiaski Cove, have been raising and eating their own rabbits for three years now, and have had as many as 36 rabbits in their backyard at one time.

They not only eat the rabbits themselves, but often trade rabbits for fish or other food. The rabbits feed on wild greens and alfalfa, and, according to Jenny, are 'nice animals', and 'really good' eating.

Rabbits also give a high yield of meat per pound, and since more and more people are starting to raise them at home, for eating, we've featured the following rabbit dishes. The taste is similar to chicken, but the amount of meat on a rabbit leg is astounding ... and delicious!

ROAST RABBIT WITH MUSHROOMS

Oven Temp.: 375°

1 whole rabbit, approx. 2½ lbs., quartered
garlic cloves
1 c. chopped onion
1 c. chopped mushrooms (Quadra's Chanterelles)
oregano to taste
thyme to taste
summer savory to taste
salt
1½ c. hot water
½ c. wine (optional)

Rub rabbit with a little salt and a clove of garlic. Saute chopped onion, garlic and mushrooms, until onions are golden. Add spices to taste. Add 1½ cups hot water to pan and ½ cup red wine (optional). Homemade blackberry is great, Cooking Burgandy is fine.

Pour over rabbit pieces, cover and bake approximately 2½ to 3 hours. When done, the hind leg should feel really tender to a fork, remove rabbit. Put the liquid over heat and add 2 cups white sauce to make a good gravy.

White Sauce:
4 tbsp. butter
4 heaping tbsp. flour
2 c. milk or 1 c. milk and 1 c. vegetable water

Melt butter. Gradually add milk to flour, mix carefully for a smooth paste. Add 1 more c. milk or vegetable water. Stir in melted butter. Heat and stir until thick. Add to rabbit liquid.

Jenny Calver

RABBIT STEW

This is the best way to cook older rabbits to ensure tender meat.

1 rabbit, chopped
1 tsp. salt
oregano
thyme
summer savory
onion
garlic
celery leaves, chopped
carrots
potato
turnip
broccoli
cauliflower

Chop rabbit up with a cleaver. Cover with water and add salt and seasonings to taste. Simmer for three hours or until meat falls off the bones. Remove bones. Add small diced vegetables. Boil 15 minutes.

Jenny Calver

RABBIT PIE

Oven Temp.: 425°

pastry for 2 crust pie (whole wheat with cornmeal
   is good)
potato
carrot
broccoli
celery
salt and pepper
oregano
summer savory
tarragon
onion
garlic
2 c. rabbit stock
flour for thickening

Stew a rabbit as for Rabbit Stew. Cut meat up into bite
size pieces. Add small diced cooked vegetables. The
mixture should be half rabbit and half vegetables. Add
seasonings to taste.

Saute onion and garlic. Add stock, thicken with flour.

Line pie pan or square cake pan with the pastry. Put in
mixed rabbit and vegetables. Pour the gravy over pie. Put
on top crust. Bake until brown and bubbly.

Jenny Calver

RABBIT STEWED IN WHITE WINE SAUCE

Serves: 4-6

2½-3 lb. fresh rabbit or defrosted frozen rabbit,
   cut in serving pieces.
1 c. dry white wine
2 tbsp. white wine vinegar
¼ c. olive oil
1 onion, thinly sliced
½ tsp. dried thyme
1 bay leaf, crumbled
2 tsp. finely chopped fresh parsley
½ tsp. salt
freshly ground pepper
¼ lb. lean salt pork, diced
2 c. water

1 tbsp. butter
12-16 peeled white onions, about 1 inch in
   diameter
3 tbsp. finely chopped shallots
½ tsp. finely chopped garlic
2 tbsp. flour
1½ c. beef stock, fresh or canned
bouquet garni made of 4 parsley sprigs and 1 bay
   leaf, tied together

Combine ½ c. of the wine, 1 tbsp. wine vinegar, olive oil, the sliced onion, thyme, bay leaf, parsley salt and pepper for the marinade in a shallow baking dish or casserole. Marinate the rabbit 6 hours at room temp., 12 to 24 hours refrigerated. Turn the pieces every few hours.

Simmer the pork dice in 2 cups of water for 5 minutes; drain and pat dry with paper towels. In a heavy 10-12 inch skillet, melt 1 tbsp. butter over moderate heat and in it brown the pork dice until they are crisp and golden. Set the pork aside and pour most of the fat into a bowl, leaving just a film on the bottom of the skillet. Brown the onions in fat left in the skillet, then transfer them to a bowl.

Remove the rabbit from the marinade and dry it with paper towels. Reserve the marinade. Brown the rabbit in the skillet, adding more fat as needed, then transfer the pieces to a heavy flameproof 2-3 quart casserole. Pour off almost all the fat from the skillet, add the shallots and garlic and cook, stirring constantly, for 2 minutes. Stir in the flour and cook, stirring over low heat 1 minute. Remove from heat and pour in the remaining ½ c. wine and stock, stirring constantly. Cook over moderate heat, stirring until the sauce thickens. Then pour it over the rabbit and add 'bouquet garni', reserved marinade and browned pork dice.

Bring stew to a boil on top of the stove, cover and cook on the middle shelf of the oven for 40 minutes. Gently stir in the onions and cook for another 20 minutes, or until the rabbit is tender when pierced with the tip of a sharp knife. Just before serving, stir the remaining 1 tbsp. of vinegar into the sauce and taste for seasoning.

Lorna McKintuck

BRAISED GROUSE

Oven Temp: 350°

A few grouse (whatever you've got!)
oil for browing meat
flour for dredging
water
a few cloves of garlic
sliced onions
chunks of carrot
chunks of potato
salt and pepper

Skin, clean and wash grouse in salted water. Cut into pieces. Roll in flour. Salt and pepper to taste.

Brown meat and place in dutch oven or crockpot. Add ½ c. water and a few whole cloves of garlic.

Layer with sliced onion and put carrots and potatoes on top. Cover and cook for 4-6 hours in crockpot, medium oven, or on stove top, being careful not to scorch the bottom if it is on the stove.

Eva Patten

RACLETTE A LA QUADRA

Serves: 4-5

10 to 15 small new potatoes
1 lb. Havarti cheese

Steam potatoes. Once potatoes are done, slice up the cheese into roughly 2x3 inch by ¼ inch slabs. Place 3 or 4 of them, well spaced, on a Teflon tray.

Put tray under broiler in oven. Broil only for a couple of minutes until cheese is totally melted and lightly bubbling. Slide each portion of cheese onto a fork-mashed potato. Sprinkle with freshly ground pepper or your favorite herb. Serve immediately.

Russ Fuoco

Mary Pirie, who has a sweeping view of Discovery Passage from her home on Copper Bluffs, grew up in Arizona where Mexican food was a regular part of the family diet. Mary's Mexican dinners are well-known on Quadra and her Chile Relleno casserole is one of her most popular dishes.

CHILE RELLENO CASSEROLE

Oven Temp.: 350°
Serves: 4

2-4oz. cans whole roasted green chiles or 6 fresh roasted and peeled chiles
1 c. grated sharp cheddar
1 c. grated mozzarella
6 eggs, beaten

Mix the two cheeses. Split chiles open and remove seeds if you want. Lightly stuff the chiles with cheese. Place chiles in an oiled 8x8 pan. Beat the eggs with salt and a pinch of oregano. Pour eggs over chiles.

Bake at 350° for 20-25 minutes or until eggs are set. Serve hot with taco or chile sauce.

Mary Pirie

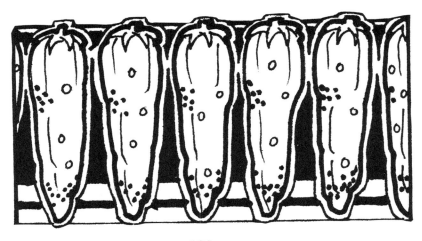

CHEESE FONDU

Serves: 4

¾ lb. Swiss (Emmentaler) cheese, grated
¼ lb. gruyere cheese, grated
3 tbsp. kirsch (or cherry brandy)
1½ tbsp. cornstarch
2 c. dry white wine
dash nutmeg and paprika
heavy dash of pepper
french bread cubed with crust
clove of garlic

also needed:
Fondu pot
Sterno (needs methyl hydrate as fuel)
Fondu forks

Rub fondu pot (or heavy saucepan) with garlic powder or garlic clove. Dredge the cheese in flour. Mix kirsch and cornstarch. Set aside. Add wine to heavy saucepan (or fondu pot), warm (on stove) until bubbles rise to surface. Do not boil.

Add cheese, handful at a time, stirring constantly in a figure 8 with wooden spoon. Keep heat high, but don't boil. Bubble gently. When cheese is all dissolved, add seasonings and kirsch mixture. Stir. Serve immediately over sterno (which keeps the fondu hot). When eating, swirl bread around to keep fondu moving. If too thick, add wine.

You need fondu forks to spear the bread on. Half the fun of this meal is sitting around a table with friends, with all the forks stuck in the cheese, as you relax and chat together. In Switzerland, fondu is known as the 'Friendship Dish' and it's a superb meal to be shared with close friends. The trick is getting the consistency just right, (like a thick sauce), not gooey and elastic, or thin and runny. Good luck and one more hint. Pepper on your plate to dunk the bread and cheese in is good. Serve with green salad, wine or tea.

Star Fuoco

140

The following two recipes come to us from Taku Resort, where former chef Jeremy Maynard served them at the Sunday brunch during the winter months. These two dishes were so popular that he chose them for us ... and since he is no longer at Taku, this may be the only way you can still get and enjoy these two brunch specialties.

QUICHE   LORRAINE

Preheat Oven: 425°
Oven Temp.: 325°

Pastry for 1 piecrust
1 tbsp. butter, softened
12 bacon slices
4 eggs
2 c. heavy or whipping cream
3/4 tsp. salt
pinch of nutmeg
1/4 lb. natural Swiss cheese, shredded (1 cup)

Prepare and roll out pastry; line one 9 inch pie plate. Spread crust evenly with softened butter; chill well.

In 10 inch skillet over medium heat, fry bacon slices until crisp and brown. Drain bacon on paper towels and crumble. Preheat oven to 425°. Spread crumbled bacon pieces in prepared pie crust. With wire wisk, beat eggs, cream, salt and nutmeg. Stir in cheese. Pour egg mixture into crust. Bake 15 minutes; turn oven control to 325°. Bake 35 minutes.

Quiche is cooked when knife inserted in center comes out clean. Let stand 10 minutes before serving.

Taku   Restaurant

EGGS   BENEDICT

Serves: 2

4 eggs
2 English Muffins
butter or margarine
4 slices Canadian bacon or cooked ham

Hollandaise Sauce:
3 egg yolks
2 tbsp. lemon juice
$1/2$ c. butter or margarine
$1/4$ tsp. salt

Prepare Hollandaise Sauce; keep warm (see below)
Poach 4 eggs until of desired doneness. Keep eggs warm. Preheat broiler. Split muffins; spread each half lightly with butter or margarine. Place, buttered side up, on broiling pan, with bacon or cooked ham alongside. Broil until muffin halves are toasted and bacon or ham is heated through. On heated platter, place bacon or ham slice on each muffin half; top each with a poached egg. Generously spoon Hollandaise Sauce over eggs.

To prepare Hollandaise Sauce:
Add egg yolks and lemon juice to double-boiler top; with wire whisk or slotted spoon, beat until well mixed. Place double-boiler top over bottom containing hot, not boiling, water. Add one third of the butter or margarine to the egg yolk mixture and cook, beating constantly, until the butter is completely melted. Add another third of butter, beating constantly; repeat with remaining third, beating until mixture thickens and is heated through. Remove from heat; stir in salt. Keep warm.

Taku Resort

VEGGIE LASAGNE

Oven Temp.: 300°
Serves: 8

2 tbsp. oil
1 c. sliced onions
1/2 c. diced carrots
1/2 c. diced celery
1 clove garlic, minced
1 1/2 tsp. oregano
1/4 tsp. celery seed
1 tsp. thyme
1 1/2 tsp. ground rosemary
1 1/2 tsp. basil
1 tsp. chili powder
1/2 tsp. salt
2 small cans tomato paste
1 tbsp. honey
1 - 10oz. can mushrooms, undrained
6 or more lasagne noodles
1/2 lb. cheddar cheese, sliced
1/2 lb. mozzarella cheese, sliced
1 1/2 lb. regular or dry cottage cheese

Saute onions in oil until transparent. Add carrots, celery and garlic and saute for 5 min.. Add all seasonings and saute for 1 min.. Stir in tomato paste, honey and mushrooms (you may need a little water). Bring to a boil and simmer while cooking noodles according to package directions. Spread a thin layer of sauce over the bottom of an oiled 9x13 inch pan. Add a layer of noodles, cottage cheese, cheddar cheese and sauce. Repeat layers, ending with mozzarella and a little sauce on top. Bake for 50 minutes or until lasagne is bubbling. Let cool for 10 minutes. Serve with crisp salad.

Sophie Gregg

143

STUFFED CHARD

Oven Temp: 350°

Serves: 4

16 outer chard leaves
2½ c. cooked brown rice
1 onion chopped
¼ c. oil
¾ c. cottage cheese
¾ c. feta cheese, crumbled
1 egg, beaten
½ c. parsley, chopped
¾ c. toasted sunflower seeds
1 tsp. dried dill or 1 tbsp. fresh
½ tsp. salt

Saute onion in oil and mix all ingredients together except the chard. Remove the stem on the chard and place about 2 tbsp. filling on the underside of the leaf. Roll up, folding in the sides to make a tight little packet. Place seam side down in a greased casserole. Cover and bake for 30 minutes.

Brenda Pulvermacher

CARROT CASSEROLE

Oven Temp.: 350°

Serves: 2-4

¼ c. peanut butter
¼ c. tomato juice
¾ c. cooked brown rice
½ c. shredded carrots
1½ stalks celery, chopped
1 small onion, chopped
1 egg
2 tbsp. chopped green pepper
½ tsp. salt

Mix together peanut butter and tomato juice. Combine all ingredients. Bake for 45 minutes or more.

Elaine Richards

BEAN'S COUNTRY POTATO PIE

Oven Temp.: 375°
Serves: 4

George Anderson collected this recipe from Gay Finch, (Bean), after having sampled it at a barn dance on the old Joyce Farm. It's easy to make and a real delight.

> **2 tbsp. butter**
> **3 medium potatoes, peeled**
> **1½ tsp. salt (or 1 tsp. salt and ½ tsp. garlic salt)**
> **1 c. shredded Swiss cheese, or cheddar**
> **½ tsp. paprika**
> **½ c. mushrooms, chopped**
> **½ c. onions, chopped**
> **2 eggs**
> **1 c. milk**
> **½ tsp. pepper**
> **2 tbsp. chopped parsley**
> **½ tsp. dry mustard**

Spread 1 tbsp. butter over bottom and sides of 9 inch pie plate. Shred potatoes in course grater. Sprinkle 1 tsp. salt on potatoes. Press over bottom and side of pie plate to from crust. Sprinkle cheese over potato crust.

Melt remaining 1 tbs. butter in skillet. Add onion and mushrooms, cook until tender and transparent. Spread over cheese.

Beat eggs with remaining ½ tsp. salt, milk, pepper, parsley, paprika, and mustard. Pour over onion, mushrooms and cheese in pie plate.

Bake for 40-45 minutes, until edge of pie is golden and knife inserted in center comes out clean. Let stand 10 minutes before serving.

George Anderson

HONEY CURRY PLATTER

Serves: 4-6

4 c. cooked brown rice (2 c. raw brown rice)
2 c. cooked and salted kidney beans or small red
  beans (¾ c. raw beans)
2 tbsp. butter
1 tbsp. arrowroot starch or 2½ tbsp whole wheat
  flour
2 c. milk
¾ c. instant non-fat dry milk
1 tbsp. lemon juice
1 tbsp. honey
2 tsp. curry powder
1 tsp. salt
oil
¼ c. sesame meal
1 medium onion, diced
2 cloves garlic, minced
2 medium carrots, diced
2 small zucchini, diced
whole cooked shrimp
sliced fresh nectarines
fresh green grapes

On a large baking platter, place the cooked rice and
beans. In a saucepan make cream sauce with butter,
arrowroot starch (or flour), milk and instant milk. When
thickened, add lemon juice, honey, curry powder and salt.
In oil, saute sesame meal, onion, garlic, carrots and
zucchini. Arrange sauteed vegetables over rice and beans.
Arrange shrimp (optional). Pour cream sauce over all.
Garnish with nectarines and grapes. The fruit makes this
dish an incredible feast for the eyes and mouth.

Wendy Walsh

MUSHROOM   CUTLETS

Serves: 4

2 c. fresh mushrooms [finely chopped]
1½ c. grated Cheddar cheese
4 green onions [finely chopped]
1 c. bread crumbs
2 eggs

Mix all ingredients together and shape into patties. Fry to a golden brown in butter.

Serve as a main dish with fresh green salad. The kids loved them until they found out they were made with mushrooms.

Diana DiCastri

PAKISTANI   EGGPLANT

Serves: 4 as side dish
2 as an entree

1 medium size eggplant
1 - 6 oz. can of tomato sauce
olive oil
1-2 garlic cloves
whole cumin, to taste
cayenne, to taste
¼ tsp. paprika
½ tsp. salt
green pepper (optional)

Cut eggplant in ¼ inch wide slices. Heat ½ inch of oil in fry pan with garlic and cumin. Put pieces of eggplant in to fry, turn once and overlap pieces as they fry. Add more oil as needed. Add green pepper.

Mix tomato sauce, cayenne, salt, pepper and paprika. Pour over the eggplant in a casserole dish and gently shake to mix. Cover and refrigerate for 1 day. Serve cold.

Cec Schnurr

SOUFFLED EGGPLANT

Preheat Oven: 400°
Oven Temp.: 375°
Serves: 8

Here is a French eggplant dish that is a welcome change from Italian and Middle Eastern eggplant recipes. It's vegetarian too and elegant.

4 medium eggplants
6 tbsp. olive oil
1 red pepper, finely minced
1 green pepper, finely minced
3 tbsp. butter
3 tbsp. flour
1 c. milk
4 eggs, separated
Salt and pepper
Nutmeg
⅔ c. Swiss gruyere cheese, grated

Cut the eggplants in half lengthwise. Scoop out the flesh, leaving the shells ¼ inch thick. Cube the pulp and drain it for a half hour. Sprinkle the shells with salt and drain upside down on paper towelling.

Heat 2 tbsp. olive oil in a pan and add the finely minced red and green pepper. Saute this for 10 minutes, until very tender. Reserve.

Melt the butter in a saucepan and add the flour. Cook for a few minutes, then add the milk by whisking it in, and cook until thickened. Remove from the heat and add the egg yolks, one at a time. Season with salt and pepper and a pinch of nutmeg. Reserve.

Dry the eggplant cubes thoroughly and saute in 4 tbsp. olive oil until soft and browned lightly. Remove and drain on paper towelling. Remove seeds and chop fine. Add to pepper mixture, season and heat. Fold into sauce, add ⅓ cup cheese. Beat the egg whites until stiff, but not dry. Fold into sauce.

Place eggplant shells in a buttered baking dish. Pile the mixture into shells (will overflow). Sprinkle with remaining cheese. Place in heated oven. Turn heat down to 375° and bake for 30 minutes.

Pat Garland

MEXICAN EGGPLANT
Oven Temp.: 450° and 350°
Serves: 4

1 large eggplant
$\frac{1}{4}$ c. oil
1 15 oz. can tomato sauce
1 can chopped green chiles
$\frac{1}{2}$ c. chopped green onion
$\frac{1}{2}$ tsp. cumin
1 can chopped olives
$1\frac{1}{2}$ c. grated cheddar cheese
$\frac{1}{2}$ c. sour cream

Cut eggplant in $\frac{1}{2}$ inch slices and brush with oil. Bake in a single layer, uncovered for 20 minutes at 450°. Combine in saucepan tomato sauce, chiles, onions, olives and seasonings. Simmer uncovered for 10 minutes.

Line bottom of shallow baking dish with single layer of eggplant. Spoon on half the sauce and sprinkle with half the cheese. Repeat. Bake uncovered for 25 minutes at 350°. Serve with sour cream.

Mary Pirie

ZUCCHINI LASAGNE

Oven Temp.: 375°
Serves: 6

3/4 lb. lasagne noodles (spinach noodles work well)
4 c. grated raw zucchini
2 c. grated mozzarella cheese

Sauce:
1 medium onion, chopped
3 cloves garlic, minced
3 tbsp. olive oil
1/2 tsp. oregano
1 tsp. basil
4 c. whole tomatoes, drained
1 small can tomato paste
1 tbsp. brown sugar
1/2 c. parsley, finely chopped
1 lb. mushrooms, sliced
1 green pepper, chopped

Filling:
1 tsp. coriander seed
1/2 tsp. anise seed
1/2 c. cottage cheese
1 c. ricotta cheese
1/2 c. yogurt

Saute onion and garlic in oil in saucepan until tender. Add remaining sauce ingredients. Simmer for 20 minutes, stirring occasionally. Turn off heat and set sauce aside.

Finely grind coriander and anise seeds with a mortar and pestle. Add to cottage cheese, ricotta and yogurt. Beat well. Cook lasagne noodles in rapidly boiling salted water until tender. Drain.

In a large, greased rectangular baking pan, layer a third of the noodles, then the zucchini, half the sauce, another third of the noodles, the cottage cheese mixture, the remainder of the noodles, and the rest of the sauce. Top with the grated cheese. Bake at 375° for 35-45 min.. (A cookie sheet underneath will catch the drips).

Sprinkle with freshly grated parmesan, if desired, before serving.

Pat Garland

ZUCCHINI OR YELLOW SQUASH A LA GRECQUE

Oven Temp.: 350°

2 small zucchini or yellow summer squash
1 large onion, very thinly sliced
2 tbsp. cooking oil
1 can tomato paste
$\frac{1}{2}$ c. water
salt
dash of red pepper
lots of basil
1 c. milk
3 beaten eggs
1 c. grated cheese

Do not peel vegetable. Wash and cut into cubes. Saute onions. Add tomato paste, water and zucchini. Cover and cook until vegetable is tender.

To make Greek sauce, heat milk and eggs, and gradually add cheese. Cook, stirring constantly, until sauce is smooth. Pour over zucchini. If you wish, you can top with grated cheese, cracker crumbs and dot with butter. Bake at 350° for 45 minutes.

Variations: Saute thinly sliced green pepper with onion, or add cooked hamburger.

Mieke Coddington

151

CHANTERELLE SOUFFLE

Oven Temp.: 350°

2 tbsp. butter
2 c. chopped chanterelle mushrooms (or other mushrooms)
3 green onions, sliced
1 clove garlic, crushed
4 tbsp. butter
4 tbsp. flour
1 c. milk
2 tbsp. sherry
$\frac{1}{2}$ c. grated cheese
4 egg yolks, slightly beaten
salt and pepper to taste
cayenne to taste
4 egg white, stiffly beaten

Saute mushrooms, onions and garlic in 2 tbsp. butter until liquid is evaporated. Set aside.

Melt 4 tbsp. butter, stir in flour to make paste. Gradually add milk, stirring constantly until thickened. Add sherry, seasonings, grated cheese and egg yolks, stirring constantly until smooth. Add mushroom mixture and mix well. Fold in egg whites. Pour into ungreased souffle dish (or dish with sides high enough to allow some rising). Set pan in 1 inch hot water. Bake at 350° for approx. 50-60 minutes.

Hilda Van Orden

NUT   RISSOLES

Serves: 4

2 oz. grated nuts
4 oz. breadcrumbs
2 oz. fat
2 oz. flour
½ pt. (10 fl. oz.) stock or water
marjoram and thyme
oil for frying
salt to taste
1 egg
2 tbsp. milk
1 tsp. yeast extract

Melt the fat in a saucepan, add the flour and stew for 2 minutes. Then add the stock (or water), salt, herbs and yeast extract.

Cook for 5 to 10 minutes, stirring all the time, Take off the flame, add 3 oz. of the breadcrumbs and the nuts. Cool and shape the mixture into rissoles or cutlets.

Beat the egg and milk together, dip the rissoles into this and coat with the remainder of the breadcrumbs. Fry in plenty of oil or in deep fat until well browned.

Eve Philips

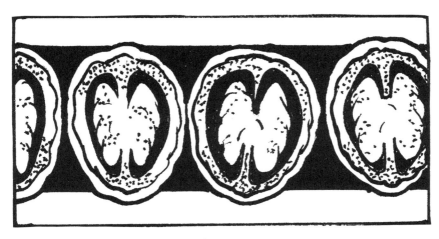

FRIED TOFU WITH SAUCE
(Goreng Tahu Deugan Sambal Kegap)

Serves: 4

6 Tofu cakes (soya bean curd cakes)
$1/2$ lb. mung bean sprouts
2 stalks celery
2 tbsp. or more onion slices, fried

Sauce:
1 onion thinly sliced
2 cloves garlic, finely chopped
$1/2$ tsp. ground chili
2 tbsp. oil
1 c. water
4 tbsp. peanut butter
$1/2$ c. soya sauce, Tamari or other
Juice of half a lemon
$1/2$ tsp. honey or sugar

Deep fry tofu in vegetable oil until they are golden brown. Drain on toweling. Put aside.

Blanch bean sprouts. Cut celery stems to about 1 inch slices, chop leaves finely. Blanch celery slices. Drain well.

Arrange tofu cubes, blanched bean sprouts and celery on platter. Sprinkle with the celery tops and sprinkle with celery leaves and fried onion slices.

Sauce: Saute onion, garlic and chili lightly together in oil. Add water, peanut butter, soya sauce, lemon juice and sugar or honey to saute mixture. Stir and bring slowly to a boil. Pour over fried tofu and blanched vegetables just before serving. Indonesians do serve this with rice, but it's delicious by itself.

Karen Murdoch

SOY BEAN STROGANOV

1½ c. sliced onions
3 c. chopped mushrooms
¼ c. oil and butter
¼c. whole wheat flour
¾ c. stock
¼ c. sherry
1½-2 tsp. salt
2 tsp. Worcestershire sauce
2 tsp. dry mustard
A few grindings fresh nutmeg
1 c. dry soybeans, cooked
1½ c. yogurt
1½ c. raw bulgar wheat or rice, cooked

Heat 2 tbsp. oil and 2 tbsp. butter in a large cast iron frying pan. Saute the onions and mushrooms until they are soft. Stir in the whole wheat flour and cook for about 2 minutes until flour has browned lightly and has coated all of the vegetables. Stir in the stock, sherry, salt, Worcestershire , mustard, and nutmeg. Cook until the mixture is thick. It will be very thick until the other ingredients are added. Stir in the cooked soybeans and cook over low heat until they are heated through. Remove from the heat and stir in the yogurt. You should have a luscious creamy mixture now. Serve the stroganov over the cooked bulgur while it is hot.

Directions for cooking soybeans: Soak in water overnight, rinse well. Boil gently until tender, at least 3 hours. If you rinse again after 30 minutes cooking, the beans will be less gaseous.

Wendy Walsh

LENTIL CHEESE LOAF

Oven Temp.: 350°
Serves: 5-6

2 c. drained cooked lentils
1 c. soft bread crumbs, packed
1/2 lb. grated cheese
1 egg
1/4-1/2 tsp. pepper
1/4-1/2 tsp. thyme
1/2-1 tsp. salt
1 small onion
1-2 tbsp. soft butter

Combine the lentils, cheese and onion. (Grind together if possible.) Slightly beat the egg and add seasonings to it. Add egg mixture and crumbs to lentil mixture and blend. Stir butter into this mixture. Put into a greased loaf pan. Bake for 45 minutes. Serve with tomato sauce.

Eve Phillips

ELEPHANT STEW

1 elephant
2 rabbits (optional)
salt and pepper to taste

Cut elephant into bite-size pieces. This should take about 2 months. Add enough brown gravy to cover. Cook over kerosene fire for about four weeks at 405°. This will serve 3800 people. If more are expected, the two rabbits may be added, but do this only if necessary as most people do not like to find hare in their stew.

Gary and Hughie

Side dishes

CHEESY BROCCOLI CASSEROLE

Oven Temp.: 350°
Serves: 4-6

1½ lbs. broccoli
2 slightly beaten eggs
¾ c. cottage cheese
½ c. shredded cheddar
2 tbsp. chopped onion
1 tsp. Worcestershire sauce
½ tsp. salt
dash of pepper
¼ c. bread crumbs
1 tbsp. melted butter

Boil broccoli until crisp. Meanwhile mix eggs, cheeses, onion, Worcestershire sauce, salt and pepper. Arrange broccoli in a casserole dish. Spoon cheese mixture on top. Stir bread crumbs and butter over cheese mixture. Bake uncovered for 15-20 minutes.

D. Heath

PINEAPPLE GLAZED CARROTS

4 or 5 carrots
salt if desired
½-¾ c. pineapple juice from can of pineapple
   tidbits
1 tbsp. cornstarch
2 tbsp. butter
½ c. pineapple tidbits

Cook carrots until barely tender. Drain any remaining liquid into measuring cup, then add pineapple syrup to measure 1 cup. Mix in cornstarch and cook, stirring until thick and clear. Stir in butter, carrots and pineapple and heat.

Sherry Peterson

158

BEET-LEAF PIE

Oven Temp.: 400°
Serves: 6

1 baked pie shell (wholewheat is best)
1 chopped onion
leaves from 6 beets, steamed and chopped
1 c. sour cream
½ c. cheddar cheese

Spread ½ of chopped onions on bottom of pie shell. Spread or drop sour cream blobs over onions. Add beet leaves; then add remaining onions. Cover with grated cheese. Bake at 400° for 15 minutes. Reduce heat to 350° and bake 20 minutes more.

Note: Spinach can be substituted for beet leaves.

Anne Gregg

TURNIP PUFF

Oven Temp.: 375°
Serves: 6-8

6 c. 1 inch cubes of turnip
2 tbsp. butter
2 eggs, beaten
3 tbsp. flour
1 tbsp. brown sugar
1 tsp. baking powder
½ tsp. salt
dash pepper
pinch of nutmeg
½ c. fine dry bread crumbs
2 tbsp. melted butter

Cook turnip until tender. Drain and mash. Butter 1½ qt. casserole. Add butter and eggs to turnips and blend well. Combine flour, brown sugar, baking powder, salt, pepper and nutmeg. Stir into turnip. Spoon into prepared casserole. Combine crumbs and butter and sprinkle over top. Bake for 25 minutes or until fluffy and brown.

Joy Bird

POTATOES ROMANOFF

Oven Temp.: 350°
Serves: 4

4 medium potatoes
1 c. sour cream
4 green onions, sliced
3/4 c. sharp cheddar, shredded
salt to taste
paprika

Boil potatoes with skins on until almost done. Peel and grate coarsely. Combine with all other ingredients. Turn into a buttered 1½ quart casserole. Sprinkle with additional shredded cheese and paprika. Bake 30 minutes, or until golden brown.

Mary Pirie

ZUCCHINI CASSEROLE

Oven Temp.: 375°
Serves: 4

3 c. zucchini, sliced
1/4 c. sour cream
1 tsp. butter
1 tsp. parmesan
1/2 tsp. salt
pinch of paprika
1 beaten egg yolk
1 tsp. chopped chives

Cook squash to barely done. Drain well. Combine next five ingredients. Stir over low heat until cheese melts and sauce is smooth. Remove from heat; stir in egg and chives.

Add squash to sauce and pour into a buttered casserole. Sprinkle with additional parmesan and dot with butter. Brown in oven at 375° about 5 minutes.

Mary Pirie

160

ZUCCHINI CREOLE

Oven Temp.: 350°

2 or 3 small zucchini
2 tbsp. butter
1 tsp. salt
1/2 tsp. pepper
1/4 tsp. cloves, ground
1 chopped onion
1/4 c. brown sugar
3 tbsp. flour
1 - 14 oz. can tomatoes, cut up
fresh mushrooms, sliced
grated cheese

Scrub zucchini and cut into slices. Put into a casserole dish. To make sauce, melt butter, saute onion and mushrooms with seasonings. Stir in flour and brown sugar. Add tomatoes, cook over low heat until sauce comes to a boil. Pour over zucchini. Bake for 30 minutes. Remove lid and cover with grated cheese. Cook until cheese melts.

Joy Bird

NOODLES BASILICO

1/2 lb. egg noodles
1 c. cottage cheese or 1 small pkg. cream cheese
1 small can chopped black olives
4 tbsp. butter
1/2 tsp. crushed basil

Put cooked and drained noodles and butter in a low oven or over boiling water while combining the cheese, olives, and basil. Toss everything gently but thoroughly, allow to heat well, and the dish is ready.

Wendy Terral

HOLIDAY YAMS

Oven Temp.: 350°
Serves: 6-8

4 large yams, boiled until tender and peeled
1 c. brown sugar
1½ tbsp. corn starch
2 tsp. grated orange peel
¼ tsp. salt
¼ tsp. ground cinnamon
1 - 8oz. pkg. dried apricots
2 tbsp. butter or margarine
½ c. pecan halves

Cover apricots with water and simmer 10 min. Drain, reserving liquid. Add enough water to make 1 cup.

Add sugar, corn starch, orange peel, salt and cinnamon. Cook and stir over medium heat until smooth and syrupy. Add apricots, butter and pecans. Bring to a boil; boil 2 minutes. Slice yams. Arrange half of yams in a deep, buttered casserole. Pour over half of apricot mixture. Repeat. Bake uncovered for 30 minutes.

Mary Pirie

NUTTING'S BREAD DUMPLINGS

½ loaf of bread, crumbled fine
1 onion chopped fine
poultry seasoning to taste
salt and pepper
¼ lb. margarine
1 beaten egg

To bread crumbs add the onion and seasonings. Melt the butter and add bread crumbs to it. Add the beaten egg then remove from heat.

Form into balls and add to stew. Cook in the lightly simmering stew or soup for 20-30 minutes.

Lavern Hollingsworth

162

Sauces
Accompaniments
&
Beverages

SALSA GUASACACA
SPICY AVOCADO SAUCE

1 small ripe tomato
1 large ripe avocado
¼ c. olive oil
1 tbsp. red wine vinegar
½ tsp. chile paste or very finely chopped seeded
fresh hot chile
1 tsp. salt
½tsp. fresh ground black pepper
2 tbsp. finely diced green pepper
1 cold hard cooked egg finely chopped
1 tbsp. fresh parsley
fresh coriander leaves (optional)

Cut the tomato in half cross-wise. Squeeze each half
gently to extract the seeds and juices, discard the skin, and
chop tomato ¼ inch dice.

Cut the avocado in half. With the tip of a small knife lift
out the seed, strip off the skin, chop avocado into small
diced pieces.

In a large mixing bowl combine the oil, vinegar, chile
paste (or fresh chile) salt and black pepper, and with a
large wooden spoon, mix well. Add the diced tomato,
avocado, green pepper, chopped egg, parsley. and
coriander and mix together gently but thoroughly. Taste
for seasoning.

Salsa Guasacaca is traditionally served with grilled
meats, but it is great with Mexican food.

Karen Murdoch

SWEET AND SOUR SAUCE

Makes: 2 cups

Simple sauce for Chinese food or as a fondue sauce.

1 c. pineapple juice
1/2 c. vinegar
1/2 c. brown sugar
1/2 tsp. salt
2 tbsp. corn starch

Mix well. Bring to a boil stirring constantly. Keep on simmer until ready to use. If red color is desired use a couple drops of food coloring.

Susan Bain

PLUM CHUTNEY

5 lbs. prune plums cooked and put through
food mill or sieve
4 lbs. chopped apples
3 large onions, chopped
1 tbsp. cloves
1 tbsp. allspice
1 tbsp. ginger
salt to taste
3 lbs. brown sugar
1/4 tsp. cayenne (or to taste)
3 c. vinegar, cider

Combine ingredients, cook uncovered stirring often to prevent scorching. When thick, pour into sterilized jars and seal.

Chutney is good with curries or with roast poultry or lamb. This one also approximates plum sauce for egg rolls.

Brenda Pulvermacher

The Kellerhals live on a quarter section in Hyacinth Bay, bordering the sea, and encompassing some of the most scenic and lovely views on Quadra. Their property includes several maple trees, a huge vegetable garden, and ocean flats where clams and oysters abound. Perhaps its because Heather comes originally from back east, but for whatever reasons, the Kellerhals have found that maple syrup can be successfully gathered out west too. They boil the syrup down in a huge caldron on their beach, and the result is delicious.

Rolf Kellerhals' 'grand-peres' or dessert dumplings are a good way to use up that maple syrup. They're based on an old French Canadian Recipe, also from back east. Here's to your maple feast!

WEST COAST MAPLE SYRUP

Early people on the coast tapped the broad leafed maple tree for syrup. With today's price of real maple syrup there is again some incentive to try this out. If you have access to a dozen or more good-sized maples it might be worth your while.

You will need:

(1) spigots. A simple way to make them is from maple branches, around ¾ inch thick when peeled. Cut off 4 inch pieces and drill a ¼ inch hole through the centre. Taper one end off somewhat. Metal spigots can be ordered from Quebec.

(2) buckets. One gallon ice cream buckets are suitable; bigger and deeper ones are ever better.

(3) some set-up to evaporate lots of sap. The kitchen won't do unless you like a steamy, drippy atmosphere in your house. We had a flat 2 ft. by 5 ft. pan made for us out of stainless steel sheet metal and then built a brick hearth for it near the wood supply.

(4) the right kind of weather. The sap seems to run only when nights are cold and days warm and preferably sunny. Late January and most of February tend to be best. A nail hole in a maple will tell you whether the sap is running. If it is, drill tap holes around 3-4 inches into your trees, one tap per foot tree diameter. The holes should be around one sixteenth or one eighth inches smaller than the spigot so that the tapered end of the spigot will hold tight. Commercial spigots need seven sixteenth inch holes. Tap your spigots in solidly with a hammer and notch them to hang the bucket. Trees seem to vary greatly. Some of our best ones produce around 2 gallons per tap on a good day, others are almost dry. The sap needs to be boiled down by a ratio of at least 30 to 1 to get maple syrup. To prevent fermentation the sap should be used as soon as possible after collecting.

If you feel like having a maple syrup party, why not try making some Grand-peres?

Rolf Kellerhals

167

PEAR SYRUP

If you're wondering what to do with all those pears and you're tired of canning, here's an easy (though potentially messy) recipe for pear syrup. It's so good that we prefer it even to maple syrup on those Saturday pancakes. Start with any quantity of windfall pears.

windfall pears
white sugar

Cut up any amount of pears. Put in pot and just cover with water. Boil for an hour (until mushy). Take off and mash with potato masher. Put into a tea towel (cheesecloth) suspended by a stick (a broom works ok) and hang over bowl or pot. Let sit overnight.

To strained juice add just over 2/3 c.+ sugar for each cup of juice. Boil solution about 2 hours, until golden brown. Watch carefully to be sure it doesn't boil over. I've had a sticky stove more than once. Put into sterile bottles.

Star Fuoco

OREGON GRAPE JELLY

Oregon grapes
Sugar

Pick berries at the beginning of August. You have to be quick, because they aren't out for long.

For every cup of washed berries, add 1/3 cup of water. Bring to a boil and cook for half an hour, then strain through cheesecloth.

Now, for each cup of strained juice, add 1 cup of sugar. Bring to a boil and boil hard for approximately 10 minutes. Jelly will appear to be thin, but don't worry - it will be set by the next day.

Pour into sterilized jars and seal.

Penney Townley

168

HEAVENLY JAM

4 oranges
2 lemons
1 dozen peaches
sugar

Slice oranges and lemons very thin. Peel and pit peaches. Add a little water.

Mix all fruit and add an equal amount of sugar.

Boil 30 minutes, seal in sterilized jars when hot.

Gloria Smith

LEMON CHEESE OR BUTTER

Makes: 2½cups

3 lemons
¼ lb. butter
2 c. white sugar
6 egg yolks
4 egg whites
or 5 whole eggs

Juice 3 lemons. Grate the rind of 2 lemons. Beat eggs well, add to the remaining ingredients, combine well. Cook in a double boiler stirring gently until it looks like honey. It will set up like custard as it cools. Use as a spread like jam or as a tart filling.

Stores about 3 months in the fridge.   Florence Dowler

BLENDED BUTTER

1 lb. refrigerated butter
1 c. oil (try unrefined safflower oil)
1 c. water

Cut cold butter into medium-sized chunks. Combine some of the butter, water and oil in blender. Continue blending until all ingredients are used. Refrigerate.

This lowers the cholestrol level, has a healthy polyunsaturated/saturated ratio, although refrigerated it still spreads easily and it helps the butter go further.

Judy Brooks

Judy Odell's party eggnog is a traditional part of the Walcan (Quadra's custom cannery) Christmas party on Quadra. She's made it for the party for the last three years, on request, and used 60 eggs for the last party. Beating up five dozen egg whites is quite the trick, according to Judy! The eggnog gets rave reviews, even from those who usually don't care for egg nog. Making it ahead is crucial, Judy says.

PARTY EGGNOG

Serves: 15-20

12 egg yolks, beaten
1 lb. icing sugar
$1/2$ tsp. salt
$1/4$ c. vanilla
8 c. evaporated milk
3 c. water
4 c. dark rum
12 egg whites, beaten to soft peaks
grated nutmeg

Mix together all the ingredients except the beaten whites and nutmeg. Fold in the whites. Cover tightly and let ripen at least 24 hours in the refrigerator. This may be stored for a few days - it improves with age. It is not nearly as good freshly made as it tastes too 'raw'. People who like a milder flavour, try 3 cups of rum instead.

Judy Odell

YOGURT SMOOTHIE

Yields: 2-8oz. drinks

1 ripe banana
4 to 6 tbsp. plain yogurt
8 oz. orange juice

Mash ½ banana in each of two cups or glasses. Beat with fork until smooth. Add 2 or 3 tbsp. of yogurt to each (quantity depends on how thick you like smoothie). Stir vigorously. Slowly add orange juice to fill cup. The less juice, the thicker the drink.

Rob Munro

TONY'S MILKSHAKE

Serves: 1-2

2 c. milk
½ tsp. honey
4 tbsp. powdered carob drink
1 banana
1 tbsp. walnuts
½ tsp. vanilla
1 c. vanilla ice-cream

Place all ingredients in your blender and mix well.

Tony DiCastri

HOW TO BOIL WATER

water
Vodka or Rye
kettle, saucepan or pot
fuel
stove or fireplace
matches or lighter

Check that the water is fit for the purpose intended. For drinking it should be colourless, odourless and tasteless like Vodka. Compare alternate sips of water and Vodka, or test it as a mixer for Rye.

Next inspect the kettle, saucepan or pot. There may be a dead spider in the kettle if you haven't used it recently, or you may have put the saucepan or pot away dirty. If so, a bit of a rinse-out or clean-up is called for.....

Put fuel in the stove or fireplace, apply a match or lighter, and make sure you've got a good source of heat there. Then pour the water into the cleaned kettle, saucepan or pot and set it in or on - or hang it immediately above - the source of heat.

Then go away, taking the Vodka or Rye with you. Remember: A watched pot never boils!

Phil Sampson

Desserts

COCONUT-TOPPED NUTMEG CAKE

Oven Temp.: 350°

¼ c. shortening
¼ c. butter
1½ c. sugar
3 eggs, well beaten
2 c. sifted pastry flour
¼ tsp. salt
1 tsp. soda
1 tsp. baking powder
2 tsp. nutmeg
1 c. buttermilk
½ tsp. vanilla

Preheat oven to 350°. Grease two 9 inch layer cake pans; line with waxed paper.

Cream butter and shortening and add the sugar and the beaten eggs. Beat until smooth. Sift together the flour, salt, baking powder, soda and nutmeg. Add to the creamed mixture alternately with the buttermilk and vanilla.

Turn the batter into the prepared pans. Bake 25 minutes. Top with broiled coconut frosting.

Broiled Coconut Frosting
6 tsp. melted butter
⅔ c. brown sugar
¼ c. cream
1 c. shredded coconut
½ tsp. vanilla

Thoroughly combine the ingredients. Heat just enough to cream. Spread over the hot cake and broil until golden brown. Watch closely, as it broils very quickly.

Deb Heath

WHISKEY CAKE

Oven Temp.: 350°

3 eggs
¼ tsp. salt
¾ c. sugar
1½ tsp. vanilla
¾ c. milk
1½ tbsp. butter
1½ c. flour
1½ tsp. baking powder
coffee whiskey syrup
1 pint whipping cream

Coffee Whiskey Syrup
1½ c. sugar
1 c. strong coffee
½ c. Scotch or Irish Whiskey

Beat eggs over warm water until creamy and thick. Beat in sugar. Heat milk and butter to boiling. Beat into eggs. Add vanilla. Sift flour, baking powder and salt and add to rest of mixture. Pour into 3 greased and floured 8 inch pans. Bake at 350° for 25 minutes. Cool cakes. Split in half crosswise.

Assemble cake a layer at a time; cake, then pour ⅓ c. syrup over, slather with whip cream etc.. Cover entire cake with remaining cream and let it sit in refrigerator for several hours.

Coffee Whiskey Syrup: Boil sugar and coffee together 5-8 minutes. Add whiskey. Cool.

Jane Dowler

The Landing Neighbourhood Pub is located just beside the ferry slip in Quathiaski Cove, and is owned and operated by Nancy and Morris Reid-Baumel.

Formerly, the Landing was a restaurant, and one of its best known desserts was the Landing Carrot Cake. Morris remembers one lady who came to tell him that she had judged carrot cakes in cooking contests in the past; had tasted dozens of them; and had never tasted one as good as the one she had just eaten at the Landing.

Now that the Landing is a pub, the carrot cake (and famous ice cream pie also found in this book) are no longer served, so, folks, the only way you can taste these island favourites is to follow the recipe given here and make them for yourselves. Enjoy!

LANDING CARROT CAKE

Oven Temp.: 350°

2 c. flour
3/4 tsp. baking soda
1 tsp. baking powder
1 tsp. salt
2 tsp. cinnamon
1 3/4 c. white sugar
1 c. oil
3 eggs
1 tsp. vanilla
2 c. shredded carrots
1/2 c. coconut
3/4 c. walnuts
1 scant c. crushed pineapple

Frosting:
3 oz. cream cheese
1/4 c. butter
2 c. icing sugar
1/2 tsp. vanilla

Grease 13x9 inch pan and dust with flour. Stir dry ingredients into bowl. Make a well and add sugar, oil, eggs and vanilla. Beat well, stir in carrots, coconut, pineapple and walnuts. Bake at 350° for 45-60 minutes.

Make frosting.

N. Reid-Baumel

CREAMY CARROT CAKE FROSTING

Makes: 1½ cups

2 tsp. flour
2 tsp. butter
½ c. milk
1 c. ricotta cheese
½ c. brown sugar
2 tsp. vanilla
pinch of salt

Melt butter. Stir in flour and cook 2 minutes. Add milk and ricotta cheese and stir. Cook until thickened. Add sugar and salt and stir until it melts. Remove from stove. Let cool a bit and add vanilla.

Robin Guldemond

The Lovin' Oven is Quadra's own pizza joint, where island folk singers and musicians are often the featured entertainment on weekends. Owner Jim Moats says that one of the most popular desserts served at the Lovin' Oven is his adaptation of an oldtime mocha cake recipe. Here it is.

MOCHA CAKE

Oven Temp.: 350°

3 - 1 oz. squares unsweetened chocolate
1 c. boiling water
1½ tbsp. instant coffee
1 tbsp. cocoa
½ c. butter (soft)
2 c. brown sugar
1½ tsp. soda
½ tsp. salt
3 eggs
2½ c. flour
1 c. sour cream or yogurt or buttermilk

Icing:
2 squares unsweetened chocolate
3 tbsp. butter
⅓ c. very hot water
pinch salt
1 tbsp. instant coffee
1 tsp. vanilla
3 c. icing sugar

Place chocolate, coffee and cocoa in small bowl and add boiling water. Stir until dissolved. Set aside to cool. Sift together flour, salt, and soda. Cream butter and sugar, and beat in the eggs. Add flour mixture alternately with sour cream and beat together. Add chocolate mixture and beat well. Pour into greased and floured tube pan and bake approx. 45 minutes.

178

Icing: Melt chocolate and butter together. Combine water, salt, coffee and vanilla. Add butter and chocolate and sift in sugar. Beat well until smooth. Cool. Ice cake when cool.

Lovin' Oven

CHOCOLATE ZUCCHINI CAKE

Oven Temp.: 325°

With the zucchini season always ahead, this is an excellent recipe as this cake is large and it freezes beautifully.

> ½ c. soft margarine
> 1⅓ c. sugar
> 1 tsp. vanilla
> ½ c. vegetable oil
> 2 eggs
> ½ c. sour milk
> 2½ c. unsifted flour
> 4 tbsp. cocoa
> ½ tsp. baking powder
> 1 tsp. soda
> ½ tsp. cinnamon
> ½ tsp. cloves
> 2 c. grated zucchini
> ¼ c. chocolate chips

Cream margarine, oil and sugar. Add eggs, vanilla, sour milk. Beat with mixer. Stir in grated zucchini and dry ingredients. Spoon batter into greased and floured 9x12 inch pan. Sprinkle top with chocolate chips. Bake for 40-45 minutes or until toothpick comes out clean and dry.

This really needs no frosting. It is moist and very tender and freezes beautifully. A superb cake!

Olive Colter & Deb Heath

179

POPPYSEED CAKE

Oven Temp.: 325°

1 tsp. baking soda
1 c. sour cream
½ lb. butter (no substitutes)
1¼ c. sugar
4 egg yolks
3 oz. (approx. ¾ c.) whole poppy seeds
2 c. sifted flour
3 tsp. vanilla
4 stiffly beaten egg whites

Combine baking soda and sour cream and set aside. Cream butter, sugar and egg yolks. Add poppyseeds and sour cream mixture. Add flour. Mix well. Add vanilla. Fold in egg whites. Lightly grease and flour a 10 inch tube pan. Bake for 1¼ to 1½ hours. Cool in pan 10 minutes. Remove from pan and cool on rack.

Mary Pirie

WHIPPED CREAM CUP CAKES

3 egg whites
¾ c. sugar
pinch salt
¼ c. whole blanched almonds
¼ tsp. almond extract
1½ c. whipping cream
¾ tsp. vanilla
maraschino cherries

Whip the egg whites. Bring sugar, salt and ½ c. water to boil to threading stage. Pour fine stream of syrup into egg whites, beating constantly. Beat cream with almond and vanilla extract, very stiff. Fold in egg white mixture and fill paper muffin cups. Decorate with chopped almond and a maraschino cherry. Store in freezer. Makes 14.

E. Hooley

180

RHUBARB CAKE

Oven Temp.: 350°

1½ c. brown sugar
½ c. butter
2 eggs
1 tsp. soda
1 tsp. cinnamon
¼ tsp. cloves
¼ tsp. allspice
dash of salt
2 c. unbleached white flour
2 c. uncooked rhubarb, chopped
⅓ c. milk

Topping:
1 tsp. cinnamon
1 c. chopped walnuts
¾ c. brown sugar

13x9 inch pan

Mix all cake ingredients (except the rhubarb) until smooth. Stir in rhubarb. Pour into a greased pan. Mix together topping and sprinkle on cake batter. Bake for approximately 35 minutes.

Robin Guldemond

APPLE PIE CAKE

Oven Temp: 350°

1/2 c. shortening
2 c. sugar
2 eggs
2 tsp. vanilla
2 c. flour
2 tsp. baking soda
1 tsp. salt
2 tsp nutmeg
2 tsp. cinnamon
4 tbsp. hot water
5 c. diced apples (peeled & cored)
1 c. chopped walnuts

Cream shortening and sugar. Stir in eggs and vanilla. Sift together flour, baking soda, nutmeg, cinnamon, and salt. Stir half of the flour mixture into the shortening mixture. Beat in 2 tbsp. of hot water. Stir in the rest of the flour mixture then beat in the rest of the hot water. Stir in diced apples and nuts. Spread into two 9x9 inch well greased pans.

Bake for 45-50 minutes or until sides pull away from pans.

This cake is a good keeper and freezes well.

Nana Richards and Dodie Richards

ICE CREAM PIE

4 c. chocolate wafer crumbs
1/4 c. melted butter
3 litres or 3 1/2 litres of favorite ice cream
1 tbsp. heavy cream

Mix crumbs and melted butter together. Press in a glass 9x13 inch pan. Put in freezer. Blend together softened ice cream and cream. Pour into pan and freeze for about 2 hours. Serve with whipped cream.

The Landing

IMPOSSIBLE PIE
Oven Temp.: 300°

5 eggs
2 tbsp. margarine, melted
1/2 c. flour
1/2 tsp. baking powder
2 c. milk
1 c. coconut
1/2 c. sugar
1/2 tsp. salt
2 tsp. vanilla

Combine all ingredients in a blender or stir until smooth. Pour into a deep 10 inch pie pan, greased. Bake for 1 hour and 5 minutes or until golden and knife comes out clean.

Crust will form on bottom, custard in middle and coconut on top.

Karen Abercrombie

LIZZIE'S HUCKLEBERRY PIE
Oven Temp.: 350°

Pastry for a 9 inch two-crust pie
2 c. huckleberries
2 small apples, peeled and sliced
1 1/4 c. sugar
6 tbsp. flour
2 tsp. milk or cream

Prepare pastry and put the bottom crust into a pyrex pie dish. Distribute apple slices on the bottom. In a bowl, stir together the sugar and flour, then gently stir in huckleberries. Spoon this mixture on top of the apples. With a sharp knife, make a few slits in the top crust, then put it on the pie. Spread milk (or cream) on top with your fingers. Bake for 1 hour.

The apples are inconspicuous in the baked pie; they enhance the flavour, and they are easier to pick than huckleberries!

Audrey Nelson

BLENDER CHEESE PIE

Oven Temp.: 375°

Filling
3/4 lb. cream cheese
2 eggs
2 1/2 tbsp. milk
1/4 c. sugar
1 1/4 tbsp. lemon juice
1 tsp. vanilla
1 tsp. grated lemon rind

Crust:
2 c. finely crushed graham crackers
1/2 c. melted butter
2 1/2 tbsp. sugar

Mix together the crushed graham crackers, butter and sugar. If the mixture is too dry add a little more melted butter. Firmly press on the bottom and sides of a 9 inch pie tin. Set aside.

Put the remaining ingredients into an electric blender and whirl for one minute or longer if all the ingredients are not completely blended. Pour into pie shell and bake for about 23 minutes. Cool and glaze with one of the following glazes. Top with whipped cream when ready to serve.

CHERRY GLAZE

1 c. cherry juice (from canned cherries)
1 1/4 tbsp. cornstarch
1 tbsp. sugar
1 tsp. almond extract
1 c. cherries

Cook together cherry juice, cornstarch and sugar. Mix in almond extract and cherries. Pour over the cooled pie and refrigerate.

BLACKBERRY OR BLUEBERRY GLAZE

½ lb. blackberries (or blueberries)
½ c. water
3 tbsp. cornstarch
⅓ c. sugar

Crush berries and mix with water in saucepan. Cook for 5 minutes, strain. Mix cornstarch with sugar and stir into the strained liquid. Cook over a medium heat, stirring constantly until the mixture thickens. Cool slightly, then pour over pie.

PEACH GLAZE

¾ c. peach syrup (from canned peaches)
2½ tbsp. cornstarch
1 tsp. almond extract

Cook together peach syrup, cornstarch and almond extract until bubbly. Arrange the peach slices on top of cooled pie and pour glaze over the top. Refrigerate.

PINEAPPLE GLAZE

1 c. pineapple juice (from canned pineapple)
1¼ tbsp. cornstarch
1 tbsp. sugar
½ c. drained crushed pineapple
1 tsp. vanilla

Cook together juice, cornstarch and sugar. Mix in crushed pineapple and vanilla. Pour over the cooled pie and refrigerate.

Janie Richards

TOFU ORANGE YOGURT PIE

Oven Temp.: 375°

¼ c. melted butter
½ c. whole bran cereal
½ c. wheat germ
¼ c. sesame seeds
juice from one orange plus enough water to
  make ½ cup
1 envelope unflavored gelatin
⅓ c. honey
1 c. tofu, mashed
8 oz. yogurt
3 oz. cream cheese
grated rind of one orange
⅓ c. orange marmalade, thinned with liqueur
  or orange juice

Mix butter, cereal, wheat germ and sesame seeds. Pat into 9 inch pie pan. Bake at 375° for 6 minutes. Cool.

Put ½ c. orange juice into sauce pan and sprinkle with gelatin. Let soften for 5 minutes, then stir over low heat to dissolve. Pour into blender container. Add honey, tofu, yogurt, cream cheese and orange rind. Blend until smooth, scraping sides as necessary. Pour into cooled pie shell and chill until set, about 3 hours. Spoon marmalade over pie for topping and serve.

Jessica Whittingham

FILBERT MERINGUE DESSERT

Oven Temp.: 325°
Serves: 8

This is an amazing dessert, one of my favorites. It is very unusual in that the texture of the meringue is almost that of a brownie. A must for anyone who loves filberts. Almonds can be used instead, if desired.

4 egg whites
1⅓ c. sugar
1 c. filberts, finely ground (can use a blender)
2½ c. whipped cream
1 tbsp. cornstarch or arrowroot
2 tbsp. cocoa

Beat egg whites until stiff and then add 1 cup sugar by tablespoons, while continuing to beat. Add finely ground filberts by folding into egg whites gently. Pour into a greased 8 inch square baking pan, and bake for 40 minutes.

Mix together the cornstarch, cocoa and remaining ⅓ cup sugar. Add to 1 cup cream in top of double boiler. Cook over high heat, stirring constantly, until cream thickens enough for stirring spoon to make a path. Cool and refrigerate until serving.

Just before serving, whip remaining cream. Cut meringue into 8 squares and place on serving plates. Pour equal amounts of the chocolate cream over and then the whipped cream. Dust with cocoa or, if desired, garnish with flaked filberts.

Pat Garland

GRAND—PERES   OR   DESSERT   DUMPLINGS

1½ c. maple syrup
¾ c. water
2 c. flour
1 tbsp. baking powder
½ tsp. salt
2 tbsp. shortening
1 c. plus 2 tbsp. milk

Heat syrup and water to boiling in a large pan. Sift flour, baking powder and salt into bowl. Add shortening and cut in finely. Stir in milk with fork just until blended. Drop dough by large spoonfuls into boiling syrup. Lower heat, cover and boil gently 12-15 minutes.

Serve hot with syrup spooned over and with ice cream if you wish.

Rolf Kellerhals

MAPLE   MOUSSE

Serves: 4-6

1 c. whipping cream
4 eggs, separated
½ c. maple syrup

Whip cream to soft peaks. Beat egg whites stiff but not dry. At the last minute mix yolks with syrup. (Egg yolks may curdle slightly if allowed to sit.) Fold ingredients together and put into serving dishes. Freeze until firm.

Joan Skogan

BAKED PEARS

Oven Temp.: 325°

4 ripe Bosc pears
1 c. maple syrup
2 tbsp. butter
½ pt. whipping cream

Peel and halve pears. Place in shallow baking dish. Dot with butter. Pour maple syrup over top of pears. Bake 40 minutes. Serve warm with whipped cream.

Very easy, very elegant!

Teresa Precious

GOURMET PEARS

Oven: broil
Serves: 2

Here is a very simple but elegant dessert. It calls for canned pears, but fresh can be used simply by baking 20 minutes in a little water at 350° , then proceeding with the recipe. Can be easily doubled or tripled.

1 egg yolk
3 tbsp. sour cream
3 tbsp. sugar or 2 tbsp. honey
1 tbsp. rum, brandy or sherry or ½ tsp. vanilla
1 can (8 ounce) pears, drained
2 tbsp. brown sugar

Mix together egg yolk, sour cream and sugar in a small saucepan. Cook, stirring, until thickened, about 3 minutes. (Store in refrigerator at this point if not used immediately.)

Stir flavoring into sauce. Place pears in a shallow baking dish and pour the sauce over. Sprinkle with brown sugar. Broil 6 to 8 inches from heat until sugar melts (3 or 4 minutes). Serve hot or chilled.

Pat Garland

APPLE DUMPLINGS

Oven Temp.: 425°

1 c. flour
¼ tsp. salt
2 tsp. baking powder
2 tbsp. shortening
⅓ c. milk
1 small egg
peeled apples
sugar
nutmeg or cinnamon

Syrup:
1 c. water
½ c. sugar
1 tbsp. butter
pinch cinnamon

Sift together the flour, salt and baking powder. Cut the shortening into the sifted flour; add the milk beaten with the egg. Roll ¼ inch thick. Cut into squares, cover each one with peeled, sliced apples, sugar and a little nutmeg or cinnamon. Wrap the apples in the dough.

Place in a baking dish; bake at 425° for 15 minutes. Remove from oven and pour over the dumplings the syrup prepared with the water, sugar, butter and cinnamon. Return the dumplings to the oven and bake 20 minutes longer.

Deb Heath

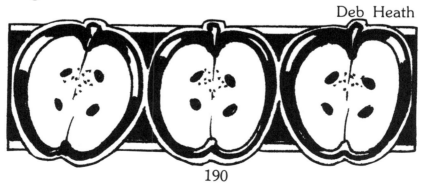

BANANAS MARRAKESH

I have never really counted how many bananas I use in this dish or how much date puree. It is a matter of trial and error each time - the right proportion of bananas to dates. Just be sure you put a very thin layer of dates or the dessert could be too sweet. This recipe comes from the famed vegetarian restaurant in Vancouver, the Naam, and is one of their favorites. These are the same directions I got from the Naam, so I don't feel too bad about passing on such a vague recipe.

bananas
dates, pureed
water
whipped cream, sweetened
allspice

In a dish with fairly high sides, put a layer of each: bananas, evenly sliced. A thin layer of date puree made from 2 parts water to 1 part dates cooked until very soft and smooth. Bananas, evenly sliced. A very thick layer of sweetened whipped cream. Sprinkle allspice generously over the cream.
Refrigerate until serving. Excellent the next day too.

Pat Garland

CHOCOLATE BANANA

1 banana
chocolate chips

Slice banana open lengthwise with skin on. Cover open banana with chocolate chips. Melt in broiler for a few minutes. Be careful not to burn chips.

Shane Hedefine (Age 7½)

191

Joan and John Sell own and manage Quadra Resort, which features six guest houses overlooking the sea in Gowlland Harbour, and offers its visitors moorage and boat rentals, guides, a freezer and a smokehouse.

Joan's green tomato mincemeat is a great way to use up all those green tomatoes at the end of the season, and, Joan says, it keeps well for a long time. When she brings this mincemeat to parties, its a recipe people always ask for, and so, to save her repeating it again and again, here it is.

GREEN TOMATO MINCEMEAT

4 c. green tomatoes, chopped small
6 c. apples, chopped small (do not peel)
1 lb. dark raisins
1 lb. currants
6 c. brown sugar
4 tsp. cinnamon
2 tsp. allspice
1 tsp. salt
1/4 c. vinegar (cider)

Wash raisins and currants. Make sure there's no stones in the currants. Put all ingredients into pot. Bring to boil and simmer 1 hour. I use sealers but it will keep in any airtight jar.

Joan Sell

MOCK DEVONSHIRE CREAM

4 oz. pkg. cream cheese
1/2 pt. (250 ml.) whipping cream
2-3 tbsp. brown sugar

Beat cream cheese until softened. Blend in cream and whip until thickened. Stir in brown sugar.

Delicious with hot bisquits and strawberry jam or any other preserves, jam or jelly.

Stevie Holden

DANISH RUM SOUFFLE

4 egg yolks
3 egg whites
1 c. sugar
¼ c. rum
1 envelope plain gelatine
¼ c. cold water
½ pt. whipping cream
unsweetened chocolate

Beat egg yolks and ½ c. of the sugar, until a light lemon color. Add rum. Dissolve gelatine in the water and dissolve over boiling water. Stir into the yolk mixture. Beat the cream until stiff. In another bowl beat the egg whites until stiff and moist. Add remaining sugar. Fold the cream into egg yolk mixture then fold in stiffly beaten egg whites. Pour into a dish and chill 4-6 hours. Serve garnished with more whipped cream and curls of unsweetened chocolate.

Hilda Van Orden

CINNAMON SOUR CREAM TOPPING

1 c. sour cream
¼ c. brown sugar
½ tsp. cinnamon
dash of nutmeg

Blend all ingredients together.
I love this served over chilled fresh or canned peach slices and garnished with toasted almond slices.

Robin Guldemond

RICOTTA FRITTERS

Make this dessert fritter batter at least 2 hours ahead and not more than 3½ hours and let sit at room temperature. A nice end to an Italian meal. They are light but rich due to the honey glaze.

2 eggs
1 c. ricotta cheese
pinch of salt
⅓ c. flour
1½ tsp. softened butter
1½ tsp. grated lemon rind
oil for deep frying
½ c. honey

Beat the eggs until light, add the ricotta cheese and salt, beating well. Then add the flour, butter and lemon rind, blending well. Let sit.

Drop by tablespoonfuls into hot oil 3 or 4 at a time. Drain on paper towelling and keep warm. When all are fried, put into a serving dish and drizzle the honey all over. Serve immediately.

Pat Garland

LEMON SURPRISE

Oven Temp.: 350°

1 c. sugar
2 rounded tbsp. flour
2 egg yolks, beaten
¾ c. milk
butter, size of walnut
2 egg whites, beaten
juice and rind of one lemon (1½ small or one large lemon)

Mix in order given in oiled dish and bake for 30 minutes.

Sherry Peterson

Camp Homewood (Pacific Coast Children's Mission) is a church-oriented year-round camp and retreat center located in Gowlland Harbour. In the summertime, more than 150 campers, counsellors-in-training, and staff all enjoy the pastoral setting of the 'harbour camp', or go off on sailing, canoeing, or wilderness camping experiences.

Marg and Alf Bayne set up Camp Homewood more than 30 years ago, and Marg's Half Hour pudding has been keeping campers warm and happy on rainy days ever since. It's a good, sweet, hot rainy day dessert.

HALF HOUR PUDDING

Oven Temp.: 375°

2 c. flour
1/4 c. margarine
2 tsp. baking powder
1/2 tsp. salt
1/2 c. sugar
1 c. milk
1/2 c. raisins (optional)

Sauce:
1 c. brown sugar
1/2 c. margarine
1 1/2 c. boiling water
1 tsp. vanilla

Mix all dry ingredients, rubbing shortening into flour. Add milk. Drop in spoonfuls into greased cake pan. Pour over the cake batter the above sauce. The cake mixture rises to the top and leaves a taffy sauce base. Bake in 375° oven for 30 min.. This pudding is delicious warm with whipped or ice cream.

Mrs. Bayne tells us that this recipe was used at Camp Homewood for years.

Margaret Bayne-Camp Homewood

Mieke Coddington, who has lived on Quadra for 8 years, came here via a circuitous route that started in Indonesia, where she was born; and included Holland, where she grew up; Yellowknife, Northwest Territories, where she was a social worker; and the state of Maine, where she got this recipe.

A friend named 'Blossom' gave Mieke the recipe, so in Mieke's family, these cookies are known as 'Blossom' cookies. Perfect for a party or special occasion.

VIENNESE SANDWICH COOKIES

Oven Temp.: 325°
Makes: 3 doz.

1/2 lb. butter
1/2 c. sugar
2 c. flour
1 egg yolk
1 tsp. vanilla
2 c. confectioners sugar
1/2 c. butter
lemon juice to taste
2 squares semi-sweet chocolate
1 tbsp. butter
nuts, coconut, coloured fancies (optional)

Cream together butter and sugar. Add yolk and vanilla. Add flour, mix thoroughly. Make small balls of dough, place on greased cookie sheet, flatten balls with bottom of a glass dipped in sugar.Bake in oven for 10-12 minutes. Remove and cool.

Cream confectioners sugar and butter. Add lemon juice. Melt butter and chocolate over low heat until just melted. Spread confectioners sugar mixture on half of the cooked cookies, cover filling with second cookie.

Dip edge of doubled cookie into melted chocolate and butter mixture and then into garnish of your choice.

Freezes very well.

Mieke Coddington

PORKY PINES (COOKIES)

Oven Temp.: 325°
Yields: 2 doz.

I wasn't ever very fond of coconut until I tried these cookies. Now I'm a coconut fan. These cookies are quite rich - a couple will do.

1/2 c. softened butter
1 c. brown sugar
2 eggs
1 tsp. vanilla
3/4 c. flour
1 c. coconut (unsweetened)
1 c. dates, chopped
1 c. walnuts, chopped

Cream butter and sugar together. Add eggs and vanilla. Beat well. Combine flour, coconut, dates and walnuts and add to mixture. Mix together well. Chill 1-2 hours. Shape into 1 inch balls and roll in coconut. Bake for 20 minutes.

Pat Garland

COCONUT TEMPTERS

Makes approx: 3 doz.

2 c. sugar
1/2 c. cocoa
1/2 c. milk
1/2 c. butter
1/2 c. crunchy peanut butter
1 tsp. vanilla
3 c. quick-cooking oatmeal
1/4 c. coconut
1 c. walnuts

Place sugar, cocoa, milk and butter in a saucepan, cook to boiling, stirring constantly. Boil 1 minute, add peanut butter and vanilla and stir until dissolved. Pour over oatmeal, coconut, walnut mixture. Mix thoroughly and beat until mixture begins to thicken. Roll into balls.

Maureen Mather

Robin Guldemond is one of those people who can juggle ten things at once, and do a good job on each of them. She has served for two years as a Director of the Nursery School, and is President this year; she started a successful La Leche League branch on Quadra; she organized a 'Mother's Group' for new mothers; she is raising two children of her own; and she still owns a bookstore in Campbell River, where she continued working herself after her first child was born.

Additionally, Robin is concerned about good, nutritional cooking, and is known for several of her recipes.

SUPER OATMEAL COOKIES

Oven Temp.: 350°
Yields: 5-6 doz.

These cookies really are super! If I bring them to a gathering, I always bring the recipe along as I always get asked for it. Kids just love them.

$3\frac{1}{2}$ c. flour (unbleached white, whole wheat
or combination)
2 tsp. baking soda
1 tsp. salt
1 c. butter or margarine, softened
1 c. chunk-style peanut butter
2 c. sugar
2 c. brown sugar
4 eggs
$\frac{1}{2}$ c. milk
2 tsp. vanilla
4 c. oats
$\frac{2}{3}$ c. chocolate or carob chips
$\frac{2}{3}$ c. raisins
$\frac{2}{3}$ c. chopped walnuts
$\frac{2}{3}$ c. coconut

Stir together flour, soda and salt. Set aside. In large bowl cream butter, peanut butter and sugars. Beat in eggs, milk and vanilla. Stir in flour mixture, then oats, chocolate or carob chips, raisins, coconut and nuts. Drop by generously rounded teaspoonfuls on an ungreased cookie sheet. Bake at 350° for 15 minutes or until lightly browned. Remove to rack to cool.

Robin Guldemond

GINGER COOKIES

Oven Temp.: 350°

¾ c. shortening
1 egg
1 c. sugar
⅓ c. molasses
1 tsp. cinnamon
½ tsp. salt
2 c. flour
1 tsp. ginger
2 tsp. baking soda

Mix shortening and sugar together, blending well. Add the remaining ingredients. Roll into balls. Do not flatten. Bake at 350° for 12-15 minutes on a greased cookie sheet.

Florence Dowler

Dorie Hall moved to Quadra in 1943, and raised a family here in the days before electricity even reached the island. Joan Hewison has been farming and working on Quadra for nine years now and has lived on islands all her life. Joan and Dorie each coincidentally entered the jumbo raisin cookie recipe as their favourite. This recipe came from an old cookbook done by the Women's Auxiliary of the United Fishermen and Allied Workers union, and, according to Dorie, the cookies have been a hit in her family for years.

SPICY   RAISIN   COOKIES

Oven Temp.: 350°
Makes: approx. 4 doz.

2 c. raisins
1 c. boiling water
4 c. flour
1 tsp. baking powder
1 tsp. soda
1 tsp. salt
1½ tsp. cinnamon
¼ tsp. nutmeg
¼ tsp. allspice
1 c. shortening
2 c. sugar (brown)
3 eggs (1 at a time)
1 tsp. vanilla
1 c. nuts

Boil raisins until mucky. Cool. Sift dry ingredients. Cream shortening, add sugar and eggs one at a time. Add dry ingredients then raisins, vanilla and nuts. Bake for 10-12 minutes.

Dorie Hall and Joan Hewison

The Richards' farm on Quadra is a well known landmark, and here Dodie and Dudley raised five children in a one-room cabin, before moving to their present modern home on the property. Dodie is one of those amazing people who has time for everything, including running two businesses...a worm farm for fishermen and a smoke house , where she turns out superb smoked salmon.

Dodie says her applesauce cookies are 'good keepers' for children's lunchboxes, and are a sure hit with children and adults alike.

APPLESAUCE   COOKIES

Oven Temp.: 400°
Makes: 6 doz.

1 c. soft shortening
2 eggs
2 c. packed brown sugar
½ c. cold coffee
3 c. flour
1 tsp. cinnamon
1 tsp. salt
1 tsp. nutmeg
1 tsp. soda
2 c. thick unsweetened applesauce
1 c. chopped walnuts and/or raisins

Beat together shortening, sugar and eggs. Stir in coffee. Sift together dry ingredients. Stir into shortening mixture. Add applesauce, walnuts and raisins.

Chill 1 hour. Drop by rounded teaspoonfuls about 2 inches apart on a lightly greased baking sheet. Bake until set, when touched almost no imprint remains. 8 to 10 minutes.

Variation: try 2 cups of mincemeat instead of applesauce.

Dodie Richards

CHOCOLATE CRINKLE COOKIES

Oven Temp.: 350°

½ c. vegetable oil
½ c. cocoa
1½ c. sugar
4 eggs
2 tsp. vanilla
2 c. flour
2 tsp. baking powder
½ tsp. salt

Form into balls, dip in powdered sugar and bake for 10-12 minutes.

Ruth Penner

PINEAPPLE SLICES

Oven Temp.: 350°

1½ c. sifted flour
½ c. butter or margarine
1 egg beaten
1 tbsp. milk
14 oz. can crushed pineapple
¼ c. melted butter
1 egg beaten
1 tsp. vanilla
¾ c. white sugar
1½ c. coconut

Cut butter into flour. Stir in egg and milk. Press into an ungreased 8 inch pan. Drain the pineapple. Pour into the pan over the flour mixture. Combine the remaining ingredients. Spread over the pineapple. Bake for 25-30 minutes. Cut into slices or squares.

Sharon Archibald

DAR'S LEMON TEA SQUARES

Oven Temp.: 350°

Crust:
1½ c. flour
½ c. medium or fine coconut
¾ c. butter
¼ tsp. baking powder

Filling:
1¼ c. brown sugar
½ c. chopped walnuts
2 unbeaten eggs

Icing:
1 tbsp. soft butter
1 c. powdered sugar
juice of a medium lemon

Cut together the crust ingredients as for a pie crust. Pack into a 9x12 inch pan and bake for 15 minutes or until lightly brown. Meanwhile mix together the brown sugar, walnuts and 2 eggs. Spread over warm crust and bake 25 minutes. Cool completely. Mix butter, powdered sugar and lemon. Spread icing. Cut into small squares when icing has set.

Dar Pirie

Phil Sampson, who has lived on Quadra for 18 years, and has recently retired from his position as Secretary-Treasurer of the Campbell River School District, has taken up several new pursuits in the last year or two, including ice skating, kayaking, and baking old family favourites like these Nanaimo bars. By the way, for those of you not familiar with our area, Nanaimo is a city on Vancouver Island, and Nanaimo bars are a well-known B.C. dessert specialty.

NANAIMO BARS

Coconut Base:
1 egg
½ c. butter
¼ c. granulated sugar
5 tbsp. cocoa
1 tsp. vanilla extract
2 c. Graham Wafer crumbs
1 c. dessicated coconut
½ c. chopped walnuts

Icing:
¼ c. butter
3 tbsp. milk
2 tbsp. custard powder
2 c. icing sugar

Topping:
4 squares unsweetened bakers chocolate
1 tbsp. butter

Coconut base:
Crack the egg into the bowl and add the butter, sugar, cocoa and vanilla. Set the bowl in a dish of boiling-hot water and stir the mixture until it is completely melted and mixed. Then add the Graham Wafer crumbs, dessicated coconut and chopped walnuts and stir until everything is completely mixed. Pack the mixture into a 6x10 inch glass casserole or into a 9 inch square baking pan.

Icing:

Cream the butter. Then dissolve the custard powder in the milk, add it to the creamed butter and sift in the icing sugar. Stir until everything is completely mixed and spread it evenly over the coconut base. Put it in the refrigerator (not the freezer) for 15 minutes to firm up.

Topping:

Melt the chocolate with the butter, and spread it evenly over the icing. Put it back in the refrigerator to set, and then cut it into bars.

Note: After adding the Graham Wafer crumbs, all stirring and mixing can be done with a Mixmaster or equivalent. If this is done the beaters and bowls will need to be licked clean after mixing the coconut base and again after mixing the icing. Count the kids and tell them who gets to lick what before starting otherwise there'll be trouble.....

Phil Sampson family recipe

OATMEAL - PEAR SQUARES

Oven Temp.: 400°
Makes: 3 doz.

1 to 1½ qts. pears
3 tbsp. corn starch
¾ c. butter
¾ c. brown sugar
1 tsp. salt
½ tsp. baking soda
1¾ c. whole wheat flour
1½ c. rolled oats

Drain pears, reserving ¼ c. juice. Combine pears, juice and cornstarch and cook until thickened. Sprinkle with nutmeg. Combine remaining ingredients and cut into fine crumbs as you would pastry. Press half of mixture into 9x13 inch greased pan. Spread pears over top and sprinkle with remaining crumbs. Bake for 25-30 minutes. Cut into bars.

Delicious served warm with yogurt or ice cream!

For variation, substitute all or part of oats with granola.

Jenny Calver

Seascape Chalet, where eight self-contained units are available to rent, is set beside the sea in Gowlland Harbour, with a tranquil view of ocean and islands. The managers are Gloria and Mickey Smith, and from her seaside kitchen Gloria offers this recipe for caramel corn, which, she confesses, she 'doesn't dare make too often' because of the speed with which it is eaten!

The recipe comes from a Ladies' Aid Society cookbook from Forrester, Saskatchewan, where Gloria went to school 40 years ago. The oldtimers there put together their best, and Gloria describes this caramel corn as 'fantastic'.

BAKED CARAMEL CORN

Oven Temp.: 250°

1 c. butter or margarine
2 c. firmly packed brown sugar
1/2 c. corn syrup (molasses would probably work)
1 tsp. salt
1/2 tsp. baking soda
1 tsp. vanilla
6 quarts popped corn

Melt butter, add sugar, syrup and salt. Boil and stir five minutes. Remove from heat and stir in soda and vanilla. Pour over popcorn, spread in two shallow bake pans and bake for an hour at 250°. Stir every 15 minutes. Cool and break apart. Store in tightly covered containers.

Hide well...these are hard to resist! You may add a package of salted peanuts to the popcorn.

Gloria Smith

HOMEMADE HALVAH BALLS

½ c. tahini (sesame seed butter)
¼ c. honey
¼ c. milk powder (skim)

Mix all ingredients. Roll into palm sized balls. Roll in coconut. Eat as is or chill in freezer. These can also be made into bars for the kids.

Reed Early

Ethel Stephens was a well-known and well-loved Quadra resident for many years, and celebrated her 93rd birthday at a party with friends, shortly before she died in 1980. Ethel's birthday parties and constant entertaining were popular social events on the island, and her braided rugs were sought after gifts. For friends' birthdays or at Christmas, Ethel would always make fudge, and we're pleased to be able to pass one of her favourite fudge recipes along to you here.

MAPLE CREAM FUDGE

3 c. brown sugar
2 tsp. corn syrup
½ c. Pacific milk (undiluted)
2 good tbsp. butter
1 tsp. vanilla

Put butter into sauce-pan and let melt first, then add sugar, syrup and milk. Heat gently until sugar is dissolved. Boil without stirring to soft ball stage. Remove from stove, beat until creamy, add vanilla (and nuts if wished). Pour into buttered pan. Cut in squares.

Ethel Stephens

Index

A
Abalone, 63
Almond Pate, Mushroom, 80
Angel Wings (Chicken), 121
Apple(s)
Dumplings, 190
in Waffles, 108
Pie Cake, 182
Sauce Cookies, 201
Shrimp Curry, 66
Avocado
Curried Crab in Baked, 71
Salad, Crab and, 70
Salad, Quick-n-Easy, 88
Sauce, Spicy, 164

B
Bagels, 100
Banana(s)
Chocolate, 191
in Milkshake, 171
in Pancakes, 108
in Smoothie, 171
Marrakesh, 191
Bannock, Irish, 102
Bean(s)
Clams with Black Bean
Sauce, 52
in Andy's Chilli, 113
Soup, Hearty Meatball, 84
Beef
Andy's Chilli, 113
Ground Nut Stew, 112
Hearty Meatball Bean Soup, 84
in Egg Rolls, 117
Leftover, Gougere Avec
Champignon, 118
Macaroni Casserole, 116
Short Ribs, 87
Skewered Meat in
Kebabs, 111
Steak Supper in Foil, 119
Beet Leaf Pie, 159
Blackberry Glaze, 185
Blended Butter, 169
Blueberry Glaze, 185
Bongo-Bongo Soup, 56

Borscht, 87
Boston Clam Chowder, 52
Bran Muffins, 105
Bread Dumplings, 162
Breads and Rolls, 93
Broccoli, Casserole, Cheesy, 158
Buns, Golden Raisin, 104
Butter
Blended, 169
Lemon Cheese, 169

C
Cabbage
Hot Coleslaw, 89
Quadra 'Use up the Garden'
Borscht, 87
Salad, Very Good, 89
Cake
Apple Pie Cake, 182
Carrot, 176
Coconut Topped Nutmeg, 174
Mocha, 178
Poppyseed, 180
Rhubarb, 181
Whipped Cream
Cupcakes, 180
Whiskey, 175
Zucchini Chocolate, 179
Candy
Homemade Halvah Balls, 207
Maple Cream Fudge, 207
Caramel Corn, Baked, 206
Carrot(s)
Cake, 176
Cake Frosting, 177
Casserole, 144
Pineapple Glazed, 158
Salad, Sunshine, 91
Cereal, Granola Deluxe, 109
Chanterelle
Souffle, 152
Soup, Cream of, 86
See Mushrooms
Chard, Stuffed, 144
Cheese
Balls, Appetizer, 82
Balls, Salmon, 12
-y Broccoli Casserole, 158

208

Cottage, and Yogurt
Pancakes, 107
Gruyere, in Fondu, 140
Havarti, in Raclette, 138
Lemon, 169
Loaf, Lentil, 156
Meatballs, Mushroom, 115
Pie, Blender, 184
Ricotta Fritters, 194
Spread, Shrimp and Ham, 64
Swiss, in Fondu, 140
Tuna and Rice Muffins, 47
Cherry Glaze, 184
Chicken
Adobo, 128
Angel Wings, 121
Castilian, 124
Company Baked Fryer, 127
Enchiladas, 114
Garlic, 127
Homemade Shake and Bake
for, 126
in Sour Cream, 128
in Wine Sauce, 125
in Wine Sauce with
Dumplings, 122
Leftover, Gougere avec
Champignon, 118
Lemonese, 120
Molded, 90
Roast, with Dressing, 129
Teriyaki, 126
Wings, Jack Mar's
Famous, 123
Chile(s) (Green)
in Bread, 102
in Enchiladas, 114
in Mexican Eggplant, 149
Relleno Casserole, 139
Chilli, Andy's, 113
Chocolate
Banana, 191
Crinkle Cookies, 202
Zucchini Cake, 179
Chowder
Boston Clam, 52
Clam or Oyster, 51
Lorne's Salmon, 15

Red Pepper, 56
Salmon, 13
Tuna-Tomato, 45
Chutney, Plum, 165
Cinnamon Sour Cream
Topping, 193
Clams
how to prepare, 48
Casino, 50
Chowder, 51
Chowder, Boston, 52
Fritters, 53
or Mussels on the Half
Shell, 50
Inauguration Stew, 57
Lorne's Cataclysmic, 49
—Mushroom Bake, 54
with Black Bean Sauce, 52
Coconut
in Impossible Pie, 183
in Porky Pines, 197
—Topped Nutmeg Cake, 174
Cod
how to fillet, 36
Fillets, Piquante, 39
Fish Kofta Curry, 40
Herb-Baked White Fish, 42
Island Fried Fish, 38
Mushroom-Yogurt Baked, 37
or Halibut Stuffed Steaks, 42
Oven Fried Fillets, 39
Coffee Ring, Jewish, 104
Coleslaw, Hot, 89
Cookies, Bars, & Squares
Applesauce, 201
Chocolate Crinkle, 202
Coconut Tempters, 197
Dar's Lemon Tea Squares, 203
Ginger, 199
Nanaimo Bars, 204
Oatmeal-Pear Squares, 205
Oatmeal, Super, 198
Pineapple Slices, 202
Porky Pines, 197
Spicy Raisin, 200
Viennese Sandwich, 196
Corn
and Seaweed, 75

Corn con't.
  Baked Caramel, 206
  Bread, Mexican, 102
  Curried Oysters and, 59
Crab
  and Avocado Salad, 70
  and Mushroom Quiche, 73
  Dish, Favourite, 70
  in Baked Avocado, Curried, 71
  in Seafood Elegant, 69
  Sauce, Creamy, 72
Creole
  Shrimp, 66
  Zucchini, 161
Croquettes, Salmon, 26
Cupcakes, Whipped Cream, 180
Curry(ied)
  Apple Shrimp, 66
  Crab and Avocado, 71
  Fish Kofta, 40
  Oysters and Corn, 59
  Pea Soup, 85
  Platter, Honey, 146
  Rich with Shrimp, 67

D
Danish Rum Souffle, 193
Dates in Bananas
  Marrakesh, 191
Desserts, 173
Devonshire Cream, Mock, 192
Dilly Bread, 98
Dips
  Bill's Salmon, 11
  Smoked, with Sour Cream, 11
Dumplings
  Apple, 190
  Chicken in Wine Sauce &, 122
  Dessert, 188
  Nuttings Bread, 162

E
Egg(s)
  Benedict, 142
  Festive Stuffed, 82
  —Nog, 170
  Quiche Lorraine, 141
  Rolls, 117

  Sea Devilled, 76
Eggplant
  Mexican, 149
  Pakistani, 147
  Souffled, 148
Elephant Stew, 156
Enchiladas, 114

F
Festive Stuffed Eggs, 82
Filbert Meringue Dessert, 187
Finnish Bread (Puulla), 99
Fish, See Seafood Specialities
  Batter for, 45
  Island Fried, 38
  Kofta Curry, 40
  Oven Fried Fillets, 39
  Sauce for, 44
  Stuffing for, 44
Fisherman's Spaghetti, 14
Fondu, Cheese, 140
Fritters
  Clam, 53
  Ricotta, 194
Frosting, Carrot Cake, 177
Fudge, Maple Cream, 207

G
Garlic Chicken, 127
Garlic Soup, Simple, 88
Ginger Cookies, 199
Glaze(d) (s)
  Fruit, 184-5
  Pineapple and Carrots, 158
Gougere avec Champignon, 118
Grand-Peres, 188
Granola Deluxe, 109
Grape Jelly, Oregon, 168
Green Tomato Mincemeat, 192
Grouse, Braised, 138

H
Half-Hour Pudding, 195
Halibut
  Baked, 41
  Creamy Herbed, 43
  (or Cod) Stuffed Steaks, 42

210

Halvah Balls, Homemade, 207
Ham
  Leftover, Gougere avec
    Champignon, 118
  Pie Extraordinary
    Morrison's, 130
  Spread, Shrimp & Cheese, 64
Herb-Baked White Fish, 42
Holiday Yams, 162
Honey
  Curry Platter, 146
  Dressing for Fruit Salad, 92
Hors d'Oeuvres, 79
Huckleberry Pie, 183

I
Ice Cream Pie, 182
Impossible Pie, 183
Inauguration Stew, 57
Irish Bannock, 102
Island Fried Fish, 38

J
Jam, Heavenly, 169
Jelly, Oregon Grape, 168

K
Kebab, Skewered Meat, 111
Kofta, Fish Curry, 40

L
Lasagne
  Vegetarian, 143
  Zucchini, 150
Lemon
  Cheese or Butter, 169
  Chicken, Lemonese, 120
  Surprise, 194
  Tea Squares, 203
Lentil Cheese Loaf, 156
Lettuce, Sea (Ulva Lactuca), 75-6
Lox, Warren's, 34

M
Macaroni and Baked Meat, 116
Main Dishes, 110
Maple
  Cream Fudge, 207
  Mousse, 188
  Syrup, 167
  Syrup with Baked Pears, 189
  Syrup with Dessert
    Dumplings, 188
Meatball(s)
  Bean Soup, Hearty, 84
  Mushroom-Cheese, 115
Meringue, Filbert, 187
Mexican
  Angel Wings (Chicken), 121
  Chile Relleno Casserole, 139
  Corn Bread, 102
  Eggplant, 149
  Enchiladas, 114
  Spicy Avocado Sauce, 164
  Style Red Snapper, 41
Milkshake, 171
Mincemeat, Green Tomato, 192
Mocha Cake, 178
Mousse
  Maple, 188
  Salmon, 24
Muffins
  April Point Famous Bran, 105
  Cheese, Tuna and Rice, 47
Mushrooms
  Almond Pate, 80
  and Crab Quiche, 73
  Chanterelle Souffle, 152
  Clam Bake, 54
  Cream of Chanterelle Soup, 86
  Cutlets, 147
  Gougere avec
    Champignons, 118
  Marinated, 81
  Roast Rabbit with, 134
  Stuffed Caps, 80
  Yogurt Baked Codfish, 37
Mussels (or Clams) on the
  Half-Shell, 50

N
Nanaimo Bars, 204
Nigerian Ground Nut Stew, 112
Noodles, Basilico, 161
Nutmeg Cake, Coconut
  Topped, 174

211

Nuts
  Nigerian Ground Nut
  Stew, 112
  Rissoles, 153

O
Oatcakes, 106
Oatmeal
  Cookies, Super, 198
  Pear Squares, 205
  —Orange Yogurt Pie, Tofu, 186
Oregon Grape Jelly, 168
Oriental Fish Sauce, 44
Oven—
  Fried Chicken, Teriyaki, 126
  Fried Fish Fillets, 39
Oysters
  how to prepare, 54
  and Corn, Curried, 59
  Bongo-Bongo Soup, 56
  Chowder, 51
  Deep Fat Fried, 62
  French Fried, 58
  Inauguration Stew, 57
  Kay's Hangtown Fry, 62
  Pat's Hangtown Fry, 61
  Rockefeller, 60
  Stew, Hearty, 55
  —Stuffed Salmon, 17

P
Pakistani Eggplant, 147
Pancakes
  Cottage Cheese & Yogurt, 107
  Saturday Morning Whole
  Wheat Banana, 108
Pea(s)
  Mia's Lovely Layered Salad, 90
  Soup, Curried, 85
Pear(s)
  Baked, 189
  Gourmet, 189
  Squares, Oatmeal, 205
  Syrup, 168
Pepper, Chowder, Red, 46
Pickled Salmon, 31-33
Pie
  Bean's Country Potato, 145

Beet Leaf, 159
Blender Cheese, 184
Ham, 130
Ice Cream, 182
Impossible, 183
Lizzie's Huckleberry, 183
Rabbit, 136
Salmon, 23
Tofu Orange Yogurt, 186
Pilgrim Bread, 97
Pineapple
  Glazed Carrots, 158
  Slices, 202
Plum Chutney, 165
Poppyseed Cake, 180
Pork
  Chops & Sour Cream,
  Baked, 130
  Homemade Shake & Bake
  for, 126
  Mu Shu, 131
  Spareribs, Teriyaki, 133
Porky Pines (Cookies), 197
Potato
  Pie, Bean's Country, 145
  Raclette a la Quadra, 138
  Romanoff, 160
Prawns
  Deep Fried, 74
  Scampi San Marcos, 65
Pudding
  Half Hour, 195
  Lemon Surprise, 194
Puulla (Finnish Bread), 99

Q
Quadra Clean-up-the-Garden
  Borscht, 87
Quiche
  Crab and Mushroom, 73
  Lorraine, 141
  Smoked Salmon, 26

R
Rabbit
  in Wine Sauce, 136
  Pie, 136
  Roast, 134

Stew, 135
Raclette a la Quadra, 138
Raisin(s)
    Buns, Golden, 104
    Cookies, Spicy, 200
Red Snapper Mexican Style, 41
Red Tide, 48
Rhubarb Cake, 181
Rice Muffins, Cheese Tuna
    (or Salmon), 47
Ricotta Fritters, 194
Rissoles, Nut, 153
Rum Souffle, Danish, 193
Rye, Jenny's Never-Fail
    Bread, 96

S
Salads, 70, 88-92
Salad Dressing (Fruit), 92
Salmon
    how to fillet, 9
    Baked Steaks in Sour
    Cream, 21
    Baked, Tomato, 16
    Broiled, 22
    Broiled Fillets, 21
    Cakes, 25
    Cheese Balls, 12
    Cheese and Rice Muffins, 47
    Chowder, 13
    Chowder, Lorne's, 15
    Croquettes, 26
    Dip, Bill's, 11
    Dip, Smoked, with Sour
    Cream, 11
    Fillets, Broiled, 21
    Loaf, 28-29
    Lox, Warren's, 34
    Mousse, with Egg Sauce, 24
    Oyster-Stuffed, 17
    Pickled, 31-33
    Pie, 23
    Poached, 22
    Roll, 27
    Quiche, Smoked, 26
    Salmon, 22
    Salmon on Cedar Sticks,
    Kwakiutl Indian Style, 18

    Sauces for Salmon Loaf, 29-30
    Smoked, 35
    Spaghetti, Fisherman's, 14
    Steaks, Baked in Sour
    Cream, 21
    Stuffed, Oyster—, 17
    Tempura, 22
    Tomato Baked, 16
Sauce(s)
    Clams in Black Bean, 52
    Creamy Crab, 72
    for Salmon Loaf, 29-30
    Oriental Fish, 44
    Spicy Avocado, 164
    Sweet & Sour, 165
Sauces, Accompaniments and
    Beverages, 163
Sausage Rolls, 132
Scallops
    in Seafood Elegant, 69
    Shrimp and, 68
Scampi San Marcos, 65
Seafood Elegant, 69
Seaweed
    and Corn, 75
    Sea Devilled Eggs, 76
    Seven Seas Salad Spice, 75
Shake and Bake,
    Homemade, 126
Shaslik, 111
Shrimp
    and Scallops, 68
    Creole, 66
    Curry, Rich-with-, 67
    Curry, Apple, 66
    in Seafood Elegant, 69
    with Ham & Cheese
    Spread, 65
Side Dishes, 157
Smoothie, Yogurt, 171
Snapper, Mexican-Style Red, 41
Soda Bread, 103
Sole, (Red Pepper Chowder), 46
Souffle(d)
    Chanterelle, 152
    Danish Rum, 193
    Eggplant, 148
Soups and Salads, 83

213

Soups & Salads con't.
  Also:
  Bongo Bongo, 56
  Boston Clam Chowder, 52
  Clam or Oyster Chowder, 51
  Hearty Oyster Stew, 55
  Inauguration Stew, 57
  Lorne's Salmon Chowder, 15
  Red Pepper Chowder, 46
  Salmon Chowder, 13
  Tuna-Tomato Chowder, 45
Sour Cream
  Baked Pork Chops in, 30
  Baked Salmon Steaks in, 21
  Chicken in, 128
  Dip with Smoked Salmon, 11
  Topping, Cinnamon, 193
Soy Bean Stroganov, 155
Spaghetti, Fisherman's, 14
Spring Salad, 91
Steak Supper in Foil, 119
Stew
  Elephant, 156
  Inauguration, 57
  Nigerian Ground Nut, 112
  Oyster, 55
  Rabbit, 135-6
Stroganov, Soy Bean, 155
Stuffing for Fish, 44
Sunshine Carrot Salad, 91
Sweet and Sour Sauce, 165
Syrup
  Maple, 166
  Pear, 168

T
Teriyaki
  Chicken, 126
  Spareribs, 133
Tofu
  Orange Yogurt Pie, 186
  with Sauce, Fried, 154
Tomato(es)
  Baked Salmon, 16
  Mincemeat, Green, 192
  Chowder, Tuna—, 45
Tuna
  Cheese and Rice Muffins, 47

  —Tomato Chowder, 45
Turnip Puff, 159

V
Vegetarian Dishes, 114, 138-156
Viennese Sandwich Cookies, 196

W
Waffles, Lovers', 108
Water, How to Boil, 172
Whipped Cream Cup Cakes, 180
Whiskey Cake, 175
White Fish, Herb-Baked, 42
Whole Wheat
  Banana Pancakes, 108
  Bread, 95
  Popovers, 106
Wine
  Sauce, Chicken in, 125
  Sauce and Dumplings,
  Chicken in, 122

Y
Yams, Holiday, 162
Yogurt
  Baked Cod, Mushroom, 37
  Pancakes, Cottage Cheese
  and, 107
  Pie, Tofu Orange, 186
  Smoothie, 171

Z
Zucchini
  a la Grecque, 151
  Bread, 101
  —Cake, Chocolate, 179
  Casserole, 160
  Creole, 161
  Lasagne, 150

ORDER FORM

Send to:
Quadra Island Child Care Society
Box 302
Heriot Bay, B.C.
V0P 1H0

Ship ___ copies of Island Cookery I @ $13.95
Ship ___ copies of Island Cookery II @ $14.95
plus $3.00 shipping and handling for first copy and
$1.00 each additional copy to:

Name ———————————————————————

Address ————————————————————

City ——————————— Postal Code —————————

ORDER FORM

Send to:
Quadra Island Child Care Society
Box 302
Heriot Bay, B.C.
V0P 1H0

Ship ___ copies of Island Cookery I @ $13.95
Ship ___ copies of Island Cookery II @ $14.95
plus $3.00 shipping and handling for first copy and
$1.00 each additional copy to:

Name ———————————————————————

Address ————————————————————

City ——————————— Postal Code —————————